THE USE OF
THE DRAMA

By Harley Granville-Barker

NEW YORK / RUSSELL & RUSSELL

PRINCETON BOOKS IN THE HUMANITIES

NUMBER 5

Contents

I. UPON THE ARTS IN GENERAL, AND
    THEIR FORTUNES IN ENGLAND   3

    Music   4
    Painting   9
    Literature   13
    The Drama and Its Educational Use   17
    Self-Expression   21
    The Receptive Side; and "Happy
        Ways of Doing Things" in Poli-
        tics or Industry   23

II. DRAMA IN EDUCATION   31

    The Sort of Play to Study   34
    Tyranny or Cooperation?   36
    The Casting of a Play: Among Ac-
        tors; Among Students   40
    The Explicit and Implicit Methods
        of Playwriting   43
    The Cooperative Task   46
    The Study of a Play Puts It on Trial 49
    The Question of Dramatic Integrity 51
    Ibsen and His "Rosmersholm"   53
    But Study Leaves the Play, as It
        Finds It, a Work of Art   58

CONTENTS

III. A THEATER THAT MIGHT BE   61

Patronage and Censorship   61
The "Commercial" Theater   64
What is a Theater?   66
The Movie   70
The Actor's Standpoint   73
The Drama of Enduring Worth   75
The Theater's Third Factor:
    The Audience   76
The Past Which is No Past   77
The Exemplary Case of Shakespeare   80
Enduring Art   83

POSTSCRIPT   87

The Coming Peace   87
Democracy in the Making   89

THE USE OF THE DRAMA

I

Upon the Arts in General, and Their Fortunes in England

THE arts in general have during the past fifty years become more and more a public concern in England. It is as well they should be, since the sources of private munificence are being so rapidly dried up by the suction-pump of the tax collector. Slowly, very slowly, we are cultivating a public conscience in the matter of the arts. Throughout the centuries they have had with us—now one, now another—their ups and downs, and, on the whole, perhaps a rough time rather than a smooth. One among them might decay and perish altogether, as did the marvelous scriptorial art of the Anglo-Saxon monasteries. Another would vanish, to reappear in a different form. The Reformation seemingly sees the end of our church architecture; but a little later comes Wren with Gibbons and his school to replace the anonymous carvers and decorators, the craftsmen of the old faith. Fresh inspiration may come from abroad, and some arts are, of course, in their very nature more internationally viable than others. Architecture and the plastic arts cross frontiers with little difficulty; music finds somewhat more, drama much more.

Music and drama—with dancing, which links the two— are everywhere, probably, the most popular of the arts. You can write them with a capital A or a very small one.

[3]

They cover a wide field. *King Lear*, the latest farce, *Rosmersholm*, *Punch and Judy*—they are all drama. A tune played by a street-corner ragamuffin on the penny whistle, and Beethoven's Mass in D are both music. Moreover I believe Toscanini would tell us that in conducting the Mass it is important to retain the spirit which animates a really good performance on the penny whistle; there is more to the Mass, that is all.

MUSIC

Music in England has had its ups and downs, but it has at no time ceased to be. How could it? In the sixteenth century and for far into the seventeenth we led Europe in the practice of the art. Some knowledge of it was a part of every gentleman's education. And even the Puritans, at the extreme of their sour tyranny, did not manage to suppress it as they suppressed the drama.* One hears of the stern old Protector, wearied and embittered, sitting by the fire in the winter evenings at Whitehall while his daughters and their friends made music for him. And its traditional association with the Church was never broken. This had survived the great changes of the Reformation; and although the Saints did succeed in closing the cathedrals and reducing the choirs to silence for fifteen years, many of the trained musicians thrown out of employ at the beginning of that time were still there and ready to take up the work again at its end (if

* But even the drama, it seems, was not so completely suppressed as we used to suppose.

[4]

the subject interests you read that scholarly and delightful book by Dr. Fellowes on English Cathedral Music).

There followed, however, a time during which—except that it was illuminated by the genius of Purcell—English music, sacred and secular both, and educated interest in it, noticeably weakened. Every art will have its fallow periods; and it is then that, the creative impulse slackening, such ties as those which bound music to the Church —the custom, in this case, of the daily choral services— will help keep it alive. Now was the time when the influence of the continental schools increased. But it is worth noting that Handel, the great foreign influence of the period, domiciled in England, was himself so influenced by English tradition and custom that he turned from his Italianate opera to develop the oratorio—a glorified church anthem.

Of the very early history of music in America I must own, ashamedly, to being ignorant. But in New England at any rate, I fancy, it amounts to little more than psalm singing and hymn singing; although it is probable that memories of balladry unsanctioned by Puritan elders could be raked up, and some young man of the wilder sort aboard the *Mayflower* may have tucked a surreptitious flute into his baggage and slipped privately away sometimes to play it. Emigrants to the Appalachians a century later certainly brought songs along, for Cecil Sharp found them there two centuries later still. There was some acting of plays in Virginia and South Carolina in the early eighteenth century. But such ungodliness did not raise its head in Boston until long after that, and then it was sternly suppressed.

It is a sorry story, that of the slow lowering of musical standards in England. The art does not, as I said, fall into absolute desuetude. Its traditional duty to the Church is a firm anchor on the one side, while on the other popular song and dance retain something of the strength of all deeply rooted, unconsidered things (if they are to die they die hard); and they feed a healthy appetite though they may stimulate no taste. But native weakness, in an art so easy of import or export as music, opens the door wide to the foreign product and its influence. The product itself is to be welcomed; only a perverted fool would have wished to stop us listening to Bach and Mozart and Beethoven because we had no equivalents of our own. The influence is another matter. Accept it supinely and our weakness grows weaker still. Creative emulation is not to be forced. But taste can be cultivated and critical standards kept high. Then, when the time comes for fresh growth, the harvest will be richer. As things unhappily were, when musical knowledge ceased to be a part of general education, critical standards in general went down. There remained, as largely there still remains, appetite without taste, while taste becomes the appurtenance of the few; and the day of the amateur dawns.

Upon more than one of our English arts the influence of the amateur has been marked; upon some for good, no doubt; but for harm also. The term first comes to mean one who cultivates a special taste for an art; and through much of the eighteenth and nineteenth centuries our best secular music, brought from abroad, owes its chief support to cultured groups of such amateurs. But by 1806, says the dictionary, the word can stand for "a dabbler" too. And from about then it is that the study of music degenerates mainly into the teaching of multitudes of middle class young ladies to play the piano—prettily enough to put Papa to sleep after dinner. The tradition of church music survives (though it too goes somewhat soft under this polite influence), and the plaintive gaieties of the village fiddler can still occasionally be heard. But by and large music in England had become a poor thing.

Within my own lifetime I have seen a change. The connoisseur-amateurs have held their ground. To their cultured dabbling the popular counterpart used to be "Ballad Concerts"; which were made up of a piano solo, the singing, in succession, by soprano, contralto, tenor and baritone of drawing-room ballads, so-called—"The Better Land," "In the Gloaming," "The Lost Chord," "The Garden of Sleep"—pretty tunes competently sung; a violin solo for variety, possibly a vocal quartet to finish, and so quietly home. In the summer in London there might be "Promenade Concerts." I remember one series of them; it was at Covent Garden. We promenaded. There was an orchestra. The conductor wore white kid gloves. Two bevies of young ladies, the sopranos in blue, the contraltos in pink, sang what were called "Vocal Valses," and sometimes we paused more respectfully, while a solo-singer shot off a ballad at us. It was not very thrilling, but the management opined that the available public would stand nothing more sternly classical. The change that has taken place is a typically English change. The promenade concerts continue; and though nowadays there are seats to be had, you still need only pay for your admission (it cost a shilling for many years), and in theory you may "promenade." But you will be wise not to try. Your neighbors will not like it. The wide space is packed by men and women who—mostly at the end of a day's work, too!—are ready to stand for a couple of hours or so, all attention, upon their two feet, listening to Bach, Beethoven and Brahms. I do not pretend that they are a highly critical crowd. There is no doubt more appetite than taste still in this love for music. But it is a love for good music; that is the point.

What has wrought the change? Education. This has not meant, of course, the direct instruction of these growing crowds in harmony and counterpoint and the like, in either the theory or practice of music. The process is indirect and slow, spreading out, often imperceptibly, and filtering down through generations. But one can date, I think, this change from the maturing of the work done by the Royal College of Music, the Academy, and other such institutions dotting the country with men like Parry and Mackenzie and Stanford at their head. They were not themselves, and they did not habitually mold, musicians of world-shaking renown; indeed, it would be perhaps the hardest part of a professor's task to persuade the overvaultingly ambitious Elgar or Holst, the too hopeful Paderewski or Kreisler in embryo that their likelier and not unworthy lot lay in a teachership at some school.

Gustav Holst, to the day of his death, earned his bread
as teacher at a ladies' college; and high and distinguished
in consequence was the standard of its music. A century
of liberal musical education, the discouragement of the
dabblers (though let them dabble among themselves if
they will), the teaching of the teachers, some study of
music for its own sake, more and more good music to be
cheaply and easily heard—the taste for it spreads, and
the national standard is slowly screwed up. It is a change
and a process worth recording, and most pertinent to
my proper subject of the use of the drama.

PAINTING

The connoisseur-amateur and the patron are first cou-
sins. The patron, too, has had his peculiar influence on
English art. With the Reformation the Church let painting slip (as it let the drama slip, too). Protestant England
was no place for Crucifixions and Saints and Madonnas.
But there, throughout earlier centuries, had been the
patron, the donor of the fresco or whatever, figuring
modestly in the corner. He had only to be brought to the
middle and enlarged; the saints were removed, and there
was the portrait. The king, in those days, was the patron
of patrons; and, the civil wars over, and he having gathered to him more power than ever before, his court became the center of art and culture. The Renaissance be-
latedly bloomed in England. But the great lords of the
kingdom remained still, in effect, kings in their own courts
too, each with his crowd of retainers, except that these
were armed forces no longer. The statesmanlike Tudors

encouraged their replacing by musicians and men of letters, designers of pageants, companies of actors and the like. Better money so spent and energies so dissipated than in rebellion. The patronage of painting in particular soon began to flow through and beyond the hands of the great into those of anyone who could afford to have his own or his wife's portrait painted—in oils; that was the correct thing. And in the eighteenth century the art was given a cachet of official respectability by the founding of the Royal Academy. Here the connoisseur-amateur had been earlier in the field. He was an aristocrat usually: witness the long picture galleries, and the portfolios of prints and drawings, now depleted, in the great libraries. The dabbler-amateur came later. With increase of leisure for the lady (compare the economy of the Verney household to life lived at Mansfield Park) water-color drawing proved to be a most delightful medium to dabble in—not oils, they made the room smell. And one did need a change from that everlasting needlework. Dabbling had its further benefits. One way at least, it can be argued, of learning to appreciate an art is to practice it a little yourself. When picture exhibitions began, the dabblers passing by could tell a bit better for their dabbling what Constable and Wilson and Crome and the rest were up to. On the other hand was this drawback. Their taste was bound to conform somewhat to the measure of their own meek achievements, and they were the less likely to give an intelligent eye to the work of the man who lived for his work alone and in a world of it. So develops a characteristic feature of both English artistic achievement and

English critical taste—for the two become, of course, reciprocal: timidity. And this still impoverishes more of our arts than one. For with it goes the wish to please and be pleased, lack of interest in principles, readiness to compromise; and these, to certain hypercritical foreigners, are the defects of some of our otherwise admirable qualities.

Painting—and not only in England—has become the art which it is easiest of all to patronize, given a respectable bank balance. You need know nothing of the art itself, nor like the picture you buy, nor—if your house has a darkish corner or so—see much of it after you have bought it. You need not care for painting at all; but pictures are creditable furnishings. If it is the work of a living artist in question, once you have handed him a check your liability is discharged. Thereafter the worst thing it can do to you is to go down in cash value. But avoid the living artist, and go to a good dealer (who has made money at the game and has a reputation to lose), and invest in the gilt-edged security of indisputable and rare old masters, and there is no great danger of that. Buy a hundred such pictures and announce your intention of bequeathing them to a museum, and you will have earned the reputation of an enlightened patron of the arts.

Not that one should mock too heavily at museum or academy, at the great, gilt, entablatured "Snooks Collection" over the entrance, or at that annual dinner party with stars and ribbons sported, and orations as banal as too many of the canvases outfacing the orators. For some such recognition is due; nobody need grudge Snooks his tribute, nor are the dinner-party speeches nor even the paintings necessarily bad. It is only that none of this has much improved English painting itself or helped to make it a really popular art. In early days the notorious English climate may have been to blame. There was a definite moral need for a Last Judgment with which to decorate the church. But even could the mayor and corporation of an English Borgo San Sepolcro have found the man to glorify their council chamber for them, would they not wisely have doubted whether, what with the damp and the cold and one thing and the other, he could look to make a good and lasting job of it. Later, painting becomes the art, and "easel" paintings the possession of the privileged few. And a young middle-class couple would, until very recently, no more think of hanging their sitting room with original drawings of their choice, or of asking the price of one at a picture show, than of making an offer for the Venus of Milo. A "work of art" was not for them —unless it was a very bad one indeed.

But this, too, has been changing of recent years; and, again, education accounts for the change. There has probably been a great reduction in dabbling. The random student has simply learned to *look* at pictures of all sorts and kinds, academic and eccentric, and to go on looking until he finds that he begins to like some of them, one or two of which he will be glad to have—if he can afford it —to live with him. It is a new and how harmless a pleasure. ("But, Mr. Turner, I never see such colors in the sky." "Oh, Madam!" answered Turner. "Don't you wish you could?") So the plastic arts also are winning their way in a socially liberal England to a status in which they may be less the dependents upon a few lordly patrons than competitive interpreters to those with any eyes to see whatever is to be seen in this many-colored, ever re-shaping world. Their economic problems have had little in common with those of the drama or of music; but each art works out its emancipation in its own fashion.

LITERATURE

Literature, likewise, has freed itself from patronage. This word has an ugly sound, I suppose, to American ears, and younger English ears may not much like it. But it should not convey mere obloquy. The practice—like the wearing of swords and the riding of horses—has had its use. In the sixteenth and seventeenth centuries an unpatronized poet—or one who at least had not the equivalent of some sinecure or fortune—would have been hard put to it to keep alive. Publishing was scarcely yet a matter of solid commerce. The famous five pounds given to Milton for the first edition of *Paradise Lost* was pos-sibly just about what to the publisher it was then worth. Less than a century earlier *Venus and Adonis* and *Lucrece*, with as much else as he could have written to fill up a volume, would certainly not have brought their author so much. (Drama was another matter; there was money in the drama. Henslowe would pay six pounds for a new play.) If the rumor were true, then, that the young Lord Southampton asked him to accept a hundred pounds "towards the making of a purchase he had a mind to" and as a tribute to his promise as a poet, surely the

[13]

transaction was creditable to both sides. Shakespeare gave what he had to give, the fruits of his genius, and Southampton (who evidently either knew good poetry when he heard it, or was willing to be instructed), dispensed a little of his more material wealth, which, as a nobleman of those days he would feel he held in free trust for his dependents. In return for such bounty public thanks were expected. They would be evidence that the patron was doing his duty. They came commonly in the form of a dedication of the printed poem. Shakespeare's to Southampton is elaborate and formal, as richly colored, as ornate as were the clothes men wore in those days. But there is nothing more servile in it than in the subscription to a letter—out of date nowadays truly—as from a man's "most obedient servant." You are not the fellow's servant, you don't mean to be obedient to him, you don't mean him to think so, and he doesn't think so. It is a form of manners merely.

But matters in this kind soon changed; the manners more slowly. Dryden, forced to do so, could, directly or indirectly, make money by his writing; Pope made quite a lot; Johnson supported himself. Gradually the patron became a superfluous ornament upon the edifice of literature (see Johnson's famous letter to Lord Chesterfield; but Chesterfield came not so badly out of the bear's hug), a prop to the ineffective author, buying with a few guineas worth of subscriptions an adulatory dedication. He outlasted his use; literature was becoming "popular," and the public was to be its only patron. But consider for a moment what the exact nature of the change has been.

If that century-past dedication, "To his grace the Duke
——" or "To the most noble the Marquis ——" was fool-
ishly flattering, at least the flattery usually ended there.
It did not corrupt the contents of the book, were the
author a man of any worth at all. Today the popular
author dedicates his book implicitly to the half-million
readers he hopes will buy it; and, that they may, it is too
apt to be riddled with flattery of their ignorances and
prejudices—which combine to make what we call public
taste. Is there such a thing? That is a pertinent question,
too seldom asked. We have not, at any rate, yet demon-
strated that appeal to the many brings a better quality of
literature than dependence on the few. And the artist's
concern is with quality.

It is, indeed, remarkable that the standard of accomplishment in English writing keeps today even as high
as it does, so small is the inducement in credit or money
to a man going into the literary market to write as well
as he can and try to write better; while the depths of "as
badly as he dare" seem hard to plumb. We have had in
England, and still hope for, writers of genius in both
poetry and prose. But too often, in the past, it was their
sheer genius which distinguished them, their imaginative
and emotional power, while the literary accomplishment
would not be very high. No matter, we said; the genius
was the essential thing. But then, alas, come the writers
who have *not* genius, and they will always be in the majority. The very greatest capacity for taking pains is doubtless a poor substitute for true genius; but it is better than
nothing, and might well be encouraged somewhat more

warmly than at present it is, and a lack of literary self-re-
spect might even better be more harshly condemned.
Compare English reviewing to French. The self-respect-
ing French critic will, as a matter of course, comment on
the form of a book, on the style of its writing, and—its
contents beside—on its workmanship and literary value.
His English counterpart will hardly be troubled by gross
errors of syntax and grammar. But each is considering his
readers; and while every educated Frenchman is expert in
French, few Englishmen know English or ever will; so
how should they care whether it be well-written or no?
Something called "Basic English" has been sprung on us
lately. It is a remarkable invention, an unexpected product of a school of subtle criticism, and—so I gather from
some of its supporters—may help implement our post-war
trade the world over. Naturally, I am all for that. Anybody will be able to learn it, from the benighted heathen
(if there are any left) to the very members of His Majes-
ty's Government; and it will be teachable, apparently, in
ten minutes or so. But I, in my declining years, shall hold
fast to useless and ambitiously literary English. Do we of
that faith need to counter the present propaganda for
"Basic" by sending out a world mission to parade foreign
streets with banners inscribed "The tongue that Milton
spake. Refuse all substitutes"? No; I believe we may do
better by staying at home and increasing and improving,
all we can, our own education in the art—the very difficult
art—of speaking and writing creditably this complex,
anomalous, ever-changing language that we have in-
herited, cultivating the great estate of it and weeding out

the ill growths. As to its writing, we need a school of stern critics, who will themselves be read. As to its speaking, something might be done by cultivating the art of the drama. To which subject I come—at last!

THE DRAMA AND ITS EDUCATIONAL USE

Drama is—it can, at least, be kept—the very simplest of the arts. "Three boards and a passion" are, it has been said, all that is needed for the performance of a play. No mastering of instruments is demanded. The painter must have his brush and his canvas, the sculptor his chisel; the writer of music demands its playing by other musicians of long training and much skill. But for the dramatist a few sheets of paper suffice; and the actor, serving him, is his own instrument. The medium, moreover, is one in which we all work unconsciously from the hour of our birth; some extra training in it cannot, presumably, be a very great matter. But there is a catch here, as, when it comes to dealing with the incalculable arts, there is ever apt to be. The human personality is doubtless, in terms of *nature*, the easiest of instruments to play upon, but, in terms of art, it can be the most difficult. For consider: with piano, fiddle or flute there are defined, mechanical limits to what can be done even by the best of performers; they are the limits of the instrument itself. With the human personality there are none, none at least that can be so mechanically defined. One may put this to something of a test by trying to transpose into the definite medium of words the many successive delicacies and subtleties of (say) the performance by Gieseking of a Debussy nocturne or of a Bach suite by Wanda Landowska. It can—at inordinate length and quite inadequately—just about be done. Now try to do the same by one of Duse's greater stretches of acting (if that is not unhappily too dim a memory now) or by the more complex interchanges of a scene from *The Three Sisters* played by Stanislawski's Moscow company; you will find it cannot be. The drama is in origin the simplest of the arts; it can be developed into the most complex.

We have hardly yet freed ourselves in England from our crooked Puritan attitude toward the drama, and oddly equivocal shadows of it can still be found falling here in America too. I used to wonder whether a that much earlier emigration might not perhaps have brought the Elizabethan theater with it. But this, of course, is ignorant miscalculation. The Puritans were already digging in while Shakespeare lived and worked and mocked at them. "Marry, Sir," says Maria of Malvolio, "he is sometimes a kind of Puritan." And daredevil Sir Andrew shrills joyously "O, if I thought that, I'd beat him like a dog." Even then they lacked not the will to suppress the theater; and later there they found—and over here they brought—the power. This they have long lost. Yet Puritan influence in other matters is by no means dead; and there are those of us who have no wish to see the humaner aspects of it die (its influence *within* the theater might come as an occasional boon). But we started the pendulum swinging. We ostracized the drama and treated the theater which harbors it as an ante-chamber to Hell. That lent it a specious attractiveness, and it gained the unwholesome flavor of forbidden fruit. Today it is a spoilt child among the arts, pampered and flattered, extravagant and presumptuous, with its true good neglected; and, although we may be caught by its glamor, we do not take it seriously. Things will never be wholly well with it— let us postulate this—until we have learnt to approach it simply, and without any self-consciousness at all.

Only recently has drama been allowed its educational status again. I say "again"; it is often forgotten how much of such service it was put to in the not so remote past. Schoolboys were always acting plays, the Universities too. At Trinity, Cambridge, the undergraduates were obliged by statute to present five a year in the great hall. The Puritans stopped that. And when, after banishment, drama did return to schools and Universities it came creeping back in disguise, so to say. It did not for long venture off the printed page: anything like acting would never have done. The study would be labeled "Greek Tragedy," or "The Rise of Blank Verse," or "The Return of the Rhymed Couplet"—anything to conceal the shameful fact that the thing being studied was really a play. And when at last it came to modern drama, the sort of play actually being acted in theaters at that very moment, and there to be seen . . . ! I am told that when George Pierce Baker (whose services to the American drama can never be too highly acclaimed) first imparted to his once revolutionary-minded President his intention of giving a course in it—on the printed page only—Eliot misgivingly shook his head. But he (Eliot) may have had a truly foreseeing mind; since once the pendulum did gather impetus for a full swing back it was to swing rapidly and far. Soon Baker was in occupation of the famous "Forty Seven Workshop" where playwriting and play-acting were practical studies; and, within a few years more, half the colleges and universities of America were following the example set, and the art of the drama was taking an often formidable place in their curricula.

A good thing, undoubtedly, by comparison with the former myopic neglect. But I have met crabbed and unimaginative educational authorities who, noting the result of letting it compete for their students' attention with less glamorous options, have found it too much of a good thing altogether. So its champions may be wise, I think, to look carefully into whatever case can be made against it, and its possibly disruptive effect upon some little world of learning.

A difficulty will at once occur from a failure to appreciate in what, precisely, the educational use of drama lies, and what its legitimate limits are. It has become today a very different and a far more elaborate business than it was when it provided those old rhetorical exercises. Educationally it can present two aspects: there are the elements of the art, and there is the developed art itself. We are apt to confuse the two. That may be because we both care too little about the elements and know too little about the developed art. Upon the playwriting side —though we shall not be dealing in detail with this— some of the educational elements are economy of writing, regard for form (drama rivals poetry here) and direct dealing with your theme. Go no further, a study of the elements of playwriting will at least teach you something of all this. Then, upon the interpretative side—which is the actor's side—there is self-expression, one of the rudiments of his particular art. Now that, with its corollaries, can be developed, I shall contend, into a very educative —and a very generally educative—study indeed.

SELF-EXPRESSION

Self-expression is a faculty with which, in your democratic country and mine, everybody expects to be endowed—and to find indulged. The right to express himself is one of the citizen's inalienable rights, freedom to express himself a freedom going with the rest. From the cradle onwards, every little democrat, kicking his nurse in the chin, and flinging his rattle to the floor, is but exercising his right to self-expression. And, since he will continue to do so in varying fashions throughout his riper years, on the rostrum or in the pulpit, on the floor of a convention or merely as one of a football crowd, there is something to be said for a little early training in the art of it, as a means to the mitigating of its cruder impulses; a benefit to his friends and relations at least this may be.

Education in our time takes a wider sweep than it did. But a generous addition of "isms" and "ologies" only resulted for a while in the omitting of certain much simpler studies; and the culture of our common speech was one of them. There were contributory causes, the chief, possibly, the extraordinary multiplication of books and newspapers, and the brighter lighting of winter evenings that let the whole family sit reading—or rather skimming—them. Human communication really seemed on the way to being mechanized (even as they say that, in another degree, the businessman, used to dictation and the typewriter, all but forgets how to *write* a letter!) , and the modern trick of mumbling your speech may well date from this.

It is worth remembering that in the last great molding of the English language it was the spoken rather than the written word which counted. If we grant Shakespeare and the Bible preeminence here, that Shakespeare wrote to be spoken does not ask argument. But the Bible also was "appointed to be read [aloud] in churches," and here, for a century or more, was the simple man's chief approach to it. How much of the rhythm and melody which go to the making of the English language today, of its beauty and power, do we not owe to those translators having had the sound in their minds as well as the sense—even to the prejudice of the sense sometimes, later scholars have discovered? And how unwilling we have been to exchange the magic of the well-known words for mere accuracy! "The morning stars sang together, and all the sons of God shouted for joy." That may not be the exact meaning of the Hebrew, but in English the very sound of it lifts us off our feet.

This question of the effective use and sensitive appreciation of our language has a wide importance. It is said to be the most universally spoken in the world. Very certainly in no other language today have words of such consequence to the entire world to be spoken, have so many of the "dooms" of mankind—to use that powerful old phrase—to be delivered. It is of some concern, then, to us British and Americans that the thousands of men and women, representing us the world over and speaking daily in our name, should be able to wield this weapon of language well, persuasively and accurately—I add "accurately" because when, as occasionally happens through its careless and faulty use, misunderstandings arise, something more than esthetics will be involved.

Good speech is, of course, a matter for primary education. Its teaching begins in the nursery, though the need for this seldom ceases there. But the adolescent will as seldom submit to continued drilling in an accomplishment that he feels sure he possesses already. So art can be called in as a more amenable aid, this art of self-expression, which is one of the elements of the art of the drama. But self-expression, as the drama involves it, asks more than skill in set speech by far.

THE RECEPTIVE SIDE; AND "HAPPY WAYS OF DOING THINGS" IN POLITICS OR INDUSTRY

It has a receptive side. The actor must study, not only how to speak but how to listen. He is, while his part in a play provides for his listening, practicing what may rather be called the art of self-*suppression*. He encourages the speaker, draws out the best of him. It is an art which in daily life few of us very assiduously practise, our minds being usually more intent upon what we ourselves mean to say next (and so may the inferior actor's be) . But that rarity, the good listener, is not the man who has nothing to say. It is, I suppose—this art of listening—in the last analysis the art of good manners; and here, certainly, is an art which it will be well should pervade our education from kindergarten to university—and beyond. I will venture on an aphorism: good manners are the necessary solvent of a democratic civilization. That is not such a banality as it may sound to this present gathering of well brought up, nicely behaved people. But I do not mean the conventional "manners" which can be learnt as is the dancing of a ballet—though I have nothing against these if they are appropriate and pretty. I mean rather the good manners which Emerson interprets as "happy ways of doing things," ways which help to ease the inevitable friction of a wearying day's work. In close-knit, comradely groups, in our colleges, regiments and clubs we Americans and English already have, it may be said, these "happy ways" as well developed as need be; not dependent upon individual likings, but upon less conscious and more lasting tradition. But what I point out is that as the world is now going—if it goes the way we wish it to—we shall need to widen the scope of these, and in an ever-increasing measure. Political democracy (which you in America acquired at a stroke, which we in England have been slowly and incongruously attaining) denies class rule, and, indeed, the rule of the elect—other than the elected!—or expert of any kind. Now, on a small scale, in a simply organized world, the unalloyed democratic doctrine doubtless works out well enough. But on a large scale, in a complex world, with experts continually called for, and men arising who make politics a whole-time job, it has for long been becoming in practice government by cliques and groups; and, in most countries calling themselves democratic, a new, motley and traditionless "governing class" has been forming, a not too pleasing contrast to the old. But the attraction to joining it—called "going into public life"—seems irresistible, whether this be thought a stepping down or a stepping up. And, having joined it, a man, so it practically follows—call him "traitor to his class," "politician," "bureaucrat," what you will—must now familiarize himself with what is a new way of life to him, and learn how to get on well with his colleagues whoever they may be. And in this he will find the art of appreciative listening a very useful art indeed.

But another influence has recently been brought to bear by the development of Industrial Democracy. This works as yet only partially and sporadically; and we still tend to think in the old terms of masters and men, or— such words having become inadmissible—of employers and employees, ranged on two sides, the one against the other. But industrial democracy, as a system, is meant to obliterate this stark division. Real differences within the body politic no system of itself can cure; and this new one may even seem to increase them, since it will certainly set them free to ferment (but sitting on the safety valve was ever a dangerous game). For it will involve the continual calling together of all sorts of men, workers by hand and brain, from the expert and the organizer to Mr. Wallace's favorite "common man," to discuss and decide, not the sort of questions which mainly go to make the programs for our present periodical political junketings, but those, only dealt with in emergencies now, which directly affect their daily lives, questions touching pocket and stomach, and likely, therefore, to be debated closely, strenuously and bitterly. It will, of course, be the realities involved which must finally count; and if an earthquake is imminent, no pills of politeness will cure it. Otherwise it is just under such circumstances that these "happy ways of doing things" should prove most needful, as between men who are *not* comrades and colleagues, who have *not* similar traditions and the same sense of values, who may begin by personally disliking each other extremely—and, for that matter, so end. But, while we await the millennium of brotherly love with proper impatience, these good manners may do something to help pull us through.

We cannot be said to have launched into this industrial extension of our political democracy, with all its cooperative implications, very wholeheartedly so far. Yet, despite disagreements, there seems to be a general and a growing sense that we are committed to something of the sort. It looks indeed as if democracy might finally prove not to be workable at all in this modern world unless it can be worked as a whole, politically, industrially, and even socially; though the full—and to some the fearful— implications of this last aspect of it have been only slowly and sporadically ripening.* Moreover, we are—without

* In England, of course, we are at present in a state, not only of economic transition but of more than usually pronounced social transition too. There are those who will tell you that today the social realities are nearly all democratic, that only a very few of the old aristocratic appearances remain. Let them add, then, that, but for food and drink, more people in this world live by appearances than realities; and add, further, that in England not only those in the upper strata of society ("stratified" is perhaps a better term than

having over-exhaustively tested it ourselves—confidently recommending a combination of political and industrial democracy to the rest of this distracted world as a certain cure for its ills, the alternative to that assumedly efficient tyranny which recently arose, a more civilized means of government, at any rate, than the Gestapo and the concentration camp. But in our happy ways and our readiness to cooperate, clearly we must cultivate among ourselves to begin with more than mere mechanical politeness and a vapid yielding to whatever opinions may be most persistently urged. We must be strong in our civilization, not weak, and the stronger if we are to abjure, and have the world abjure, the use of force. For we can hardly envisage our factories or countries, or a peaceful world itself, being run by committees composed of a few smart intriguers and polemical bullies, with a number of yes-men to make up the count. Such agreement as they reached would not be worth having. It could not last; and while it did it would be no better than a focus of moral stagnation. Differences of opinion honestly disputed and, after, every consideration to be given to the outvoted minority—this is democracy's golden rule. We need to disagree. From what but disagreement can progress spring, and respect for each other? Let us only be

"aristocratic": there has never been a permanently privileged aristocracy in England) will have preferred the old state of things, but many in the lower strata too. There was much to be said, and from divers points of view, in favor of the old order during any of its periods of stability—they never lasted long. Every man had his place in it under custom or the law. He had his work to do, and his relation to his neighbors was clearly defined and theirs toward him.

[27]

all-but certain that our disagreements cannot end in fighting—I say "all-but," since absolute certainty is only a premium upon provocation—and we can profitably cultivate them.

Yet, reduced to a mere formula, our "happy ways"—the very happiest—will prove barren. To be fruitful they must be dynamic, and they can well make some use of this art of combining active appreciation of the other man's point of view with clear assertion of one's own (self-suppression with self-expression), which is one of the constituents of that trivial and mighty art of the drama.

Do I so seriously associate the arts with these questions of high statecraft? Most seriously. On the one hand education in the arts—or, let us rather say, the inclusion of the arts in education—can be a positive help toward making a man a statesman, and a better President of the United States or Prime Minister of England than he might otherwise be. The influence of the arts in education is, of course, chiefly indirect. But it is pervasive. It gives a man poise, a point of view, sets up for him a general standard of quality. It helps refine his faculties, mature his perceptions, gives balance to his judgment. If, therefore, some understanding of Bach and Michelangelo and Shakespeare and of what they have done for the world does not make a man both express himself more effectively, and find more in himself to express, as President or Premier, or doctor or lawyer or banker—why, so much the worse, not for the arts that these men's genius glorified, but for Law and Medicine and Banking them-

selves, for Washington and Downing Street, and so for
us all. It must mean that the quality of our civilization is
by thus much on the decline.

On the other hand, from the "appreciative" standpoint;—incidentally we must not be taken in by fine
phrases. Statecraft is no mystery, simply a matter of
honesty, good sense, tradition, training and experience.
There is much to be said against the present condemning
of our public men to do most of their work in public,
photographed and radio-ed and reported minute by
minute. It can hardly induce cool reasoning and reflection, must tend to make them both self-conscious and
tiresomely oracular. Any influence of art it may show
will be of very bad art. But at least it may dissipate the
pretentiously official air which too often enwraps mere in-
competence. In any country only a selected few can be
called on to *practice* statecraft. It is the more important
that the rest of us should properly appreciate its workings,
be alive to the things done daily in the name of us all,
lest later we emerge from our complaisant confusions to
find we have been befooled and betrayed by that—as it
will turn out—*ill*-selected few. But, again, a little education in the arts, with its sharpening of the senses, its lift-
ing of standards and cultivation of good judgment, might
have helped us to distinguish in time between the sterl-
ing—if often unpopular—statecraft, and the pinchbeck;
between folly, whether dressed in finery or homespun,
and the thing that was at the moment as near to wisdom
as it is given to fallible man to attain. For art is a

microcosm of life, and the ultimate standards in each are the same.

Now, of all the arts, that which has the first educational claim on us, and the one most easily fulfilled, is this simple and complex, trivial and mighty, art of the drama. A man may never master much more than the alphabets of music and painting. But the drama is—so to say—Everyman's art; it is the direct and living reflection of life itself, and few of us can be quite insusceptible to it.

I I

Drama in Education

THE ELEMENTS OF THE ART, AND THE ART ITSELF

WE are discussing the educational uses of the art of the drama. There is in this connection the use to be made of the elements of the art, also of the developed art itself. Some of its simplest elements—concise writing, eloquently clear speaking, appreciative listening —find their place in early education, and should not lose it later; for they are seldom so fully mastered that they can safely be forgotten. With the mastery of the art for a life's occupation, whether in play acting, directing or writing, I do not propose to deal. To cover that ground fully nowadays one should include directions toward the Eldorado of the Cinema (odd that California should have seen two gold rushes within the course of a century!) and of that I know nothing. Moreover the direct study of the art itself has come to be pretty well and very variously provided for. One's passport into the service of the drama may be now a thesis for a doctorate, now a prize at a beauty show. I am concerned with the art's generally educational uses, which do not demand of the student the artist's self-surrender and devotion, but allow for the detached attitude of the scholar adding one more item to the sum of his knowledge.

I do not think, therefore, that this purely educational study would find a satisfactory home in any fully developed School of Drama, where such devotion would be the rule and little be talked or thought or dreamed of but the theater. A teacher or so might on occasions transfer from one samplings of his special knowledge, and incidentally be glad himself of a temporary release from his surroundings. But he would need to deal differently with the different sorts of students, the "devotional" and the "detached."

Yet the art must be studied, however detachedly, in its own terms. It may be doubted whether any art—though the principles of them all are probably the same—can be fully translated into terms other than its own, whether, for instance, we can expound a piece of music or a picture in words and hope to convey its essential quality. That will lie in the color and pattern or in the sound, and must be sought there. Equally, drama must be studied, as far as possible, in terms of drama (and as little as possible, you may pertinently interpose, by means of disquisitions upon it, such as this). But words are at least a part of its proper medium, and commonly the most important part. Moreover, drama is peculiarly suited to class study. And the methods of a class of senior students (a seminar, as it is sometimes called) can well resemble up to a point the rehearsals by a company of actors for a performance of a play—which will be its true completion.

The patent difference, as I see it, between the two approaches should be that a class of students will stop definitely short of putting the play into action, whereas a company of actors is from the beginning headed toward this. Every play involves action and even conflict, though it need not be physical action or physical conflict—which will, indeed, not take us dramatically very far. A knocks down B, who is rescued by C, who then knocks down A; there are not many possible variations upon that. *Punch and Judy* is the thoroughgoing play of action. The violent dramas in which our ancestors delighted usually contained a fight or two. The need for action of some sort is asserted in the convention of the French *scène-a-faire*. But it may be moral action; moral conflict, as in Ibsen's *Rosmersholm*; it may concern a man's inward struggles, as in *Hamlet*; or, as in Greek tragedy, his strife with fate and the gods. And generally speaking, the more mature a play's art the less is its action likely to depend upon either physical conflict or accident. Consider Shakespeare's artistic development, physical action being one of the dominant conventions of his theater, and he not the man deliberately to discard convention. Note, then, how in such a mature tragedy as *Macbeth*, he relegates its physical action to second place. Of murders and killings there are, I think, no less than ten; yet all but two are contrived off stage. Nor is it by the bodily death of its two splendid sinners that justice is done, but in the slower and more torturing death of their souls. *Macbeth* is above all a metaphysical—and in that an essentially poetic—tragedy.

Plainly, the least likely sort of play for study will be one in which physical action has the larger share, in which we must come to it the sooner. Here the trained actor has the advantage of the student. With him understanding and expression tend to go hand in hand. Indeed, with the over-practiced actor, expression may sometimes outrun understanding, and effects be produced of no explicable cause. We must not, incidentally, be positive in such cases that there *is* no cause. An actor of Hamlet, when he sees his father's ghost, may be able to express by intuition a process of feeling which he cannot at the moment—if ever he could—explain. The artist knows royal roads. But they are not for the student—nor too exclusively for the artist—to rely on. The student has to learn to understand, and to make his understanding clear, first to himself, and then, in this class work, to his fellow-students.

THE SORT OF PLAY TO STUDY

The likeliest sort of play for study will be the meta-physically turned play, since at that the student can for longest keep closest to the actor's method, studying the art in its own terms. Nor does the division between the two come merely because at some time the actor must "go into action," so to say, while the student is to stop short of the captivating—the too captivating—process of presenting the play upon a stage. For it will come when, earlier than this, the actors begin to change their own student-critical attitude, and surrender themselves wholly to the play and their parts in it; and that the student need never do. He must remain detached. And the process of his study may be described as an attempted resolving of the play into its constituents, a painstaking reversal of the process by which the dramatist has put it together and given it life. The ultimate secret of the life in it may

[34]

not thereby be disclosed. We need to gather humbly round any dissecting table, and always to resist the temptation—it besets the uncreative mind—to pick a work of art to pieces and put it together again, reshaped to please ourselves. The student may indeed with advantage temporarily borrow the actor's intuition—travel a short way along the royal road—since we want him to gain not a mere bookish understanding, but a lively appreciation of the play. We have only to take care that, in adolescence at least, he should not be lured too far, and away from all solider studies by this siren among the arts. Here we have, then, what should be, I contend, the decisive differences between the actor's way of work and the student's. The actor first learns all he can of the play, then goes ahead to lose himself in it, to identify himself with his particular part in it. The student and his fellows never so lose themselves; they are there rather to equip themselves as its ideal audience, sensitive, appreciative, but knowledgeable and critical. And that is much.

I do not suggest rules for the running of such a class; they will come to vary with the play to be studied and the quality of the students. I envisage some professor or instructor guiding the proceedings. I do not liken him to a director or a producer of the play, there being no production in prospect; and he will be, from the beginning, one may suppose, readier to elicit his students' opinions upon the work in hand than to impress them with his own. Or am I wrong in that?

TYRANNY OR COOPERATION?

The directing of plays has become, within the last few generations, something of a tyranny—I speak as one who has sinned; the conducting of orchestral music also. In the matter of plays here was at first a needed corrective to the lack of cohesion among the actors and the slap-dash carelessness into which all staging had fallen. It was, perhaps, a small part of that wider reaction against every sort of individualism, against our old reliance on spontaneous cooperation, of which we became conscious toward the end of the last century, and against which—if the lesson has been learnt—we hopefully look for counter reaction now. Upon music-making and drama and weightier matters than these a tyrant could beneficently impose fresh ideas. Here was rescue from lazy-mindedness and a counterpoise to complexities and confusions. A single voice, silencing the rest; then, at least, we could get on with the job, could go ahead. "Whither?" was a question perhaps too seldom asked; and the dictatorial process itself is hardly educational. Upon the performing of a play or a symphony the immediate effect of this single voice may be brilliant; but, thoughtlessly obeyed, it is likely only to lead its hearers in the long run to the extremes of stupid efficiency—which is the deadest of dead ends. And something of the kind will be as true of the running of a newspaper or a factory, or the government of a city or a country. Our class, at least, on education bent, will have no use for a dictator; and its chairman—professor, instructor, director, whatever he be—will be expected to hold his reins with a very light hand.

[36]

We shall be wise to borrow as many of the actor's methods as can be made to suit us. The best play director is he who ostensibly does least, not most. Some single governing *idea* the production of a play must have, and if the director is the author's vicegerent, it had better be his. But the actors are not puppets; and since, for the performance at least, they will have to be let go from leading strings, the less they are tied by them at all the better. There is a story of Ellen Terry, one of the few actresses of her time in whom some flame of genius burned. She once found herself in the hands of a notoriously authoritative stage-director. He gave her minute directions for the acting of a short stretch of a certain scene. She docilely repeated them. "Yes, Mr. Blank, I think I understand. I am to move here, and touch this, and to look there. And I do that and that and that. And then," she added sweetly, "I must do that little bit extra, mustn't I, for which it is that I'm to play the part?"

With every art, of course, it is that "little bit extra" which finally counts, and what the artist inexplicably *is* besides what he does. But with the actor this is most paradoxically so. His art, fully developed, is a veritable invitation to egoism, but at the price of discarding the ego altogether. He is asked, not so much to assume another personality, as to interpret a character of an author's creating in terms of his own. To do this he may need to draw upon all his resources, appreciative, emotional, plastic, to magnify himself to the utmost. Yet the character remains the author's, and while the actor is interpreting it we should forget about him. It is a hall-mark of the quality of his performance that we do. There is a delicate but distinct difference between the art of an actor giving himself *to* his part and that of one who exploits himself *in* his part, and the sensitive critic of acting will quickly discern it.

Acting is an art of collaboration—even as life is. The dramatist gives the actors a scheme of characters, more or less detailed. To it the actors bring themselves, realizing it physically, psychologically, emotionally, and setting it in action. The content and importance of the contribution each party makes will vary much—again, as in life. But all collaboration is hard to evaluate. A deed of partnership dealing with the most material matters must still leave the will to make it work undefined; and the partnership between dramatist and actor veritably approaches the mystic. The actor may bring much to little, as, seemingly, did Joseph Jefferson to *Rip van Winkle,* or Henry Irving to a poor play named *The Bells.* He may bring little to much (the disappointed and opinionated dramatist's complaint of his actors) or much to more. And while there have been a thousand Hamlets bad and good, one Hamlet remains.

Actors collaborate with each other also; and here, too, is a part of their art from which students can very profitably borrow ideas. It brings us to considering again that "happy way of doing things," which is in its kind to help us, perhaps, to follow the ever more necessarily cooperative path of our democracies in the making. The scope and subtlety of the collaboration between the actors in a first-rate performance of a first-rate play is seldom fully appreciated, even seldomer put on record, if only because, as we said of acting and art as a whole, it is hard to reduce it to terms other than its own. The overt teamwork of nicely dovetailed speech and movement is a matter of skill and practice and is easily appraised. What is not is the dialogue left unspoken, and the larger, the psychological structure of the play. For every ten lines the dramatist writes that the actors are to speak he may leave a hundred unwritten. If he did not confine himself to setting down the essential and significant his play would never be finished. But the purport of what stays unwritten the actor must nevertheless be able to divine; this is not so much rejected matter as scaffolding used for the play's building, only to be discarded on its completion. Actors, preparing their performance, are, in a way, repeating that process, our students a part of it likewise. Therefore they must divine what it was (an aspect, this, of their collaboration with the author), and by some means agree upon it among themselves (their collaboration with each other). In all highly organized drama the amount of the unwritten will exceed the amount written by much, so the field in which the actors' imagination can operate will be wide. And in this, perhaps, the technique of the theater reaches its maturest development, the art of the actor most fruitfully supplementing the dramatist's art. The actor interprets, and, as in any partnership, honesty of purpose is presumed. But the dramatist learns to give the actor material so contrived that only willfully can he misinterpret it; and, for the rest, he leaves him free—he encourages him—to enrich his interpretation to the full extent of his own imaginative power.

Creative interpretation, self-expression to the full with the "self" sacrificed; these paradoxes resolved, add a common loyalty to the play, coupled with loyalty to each other, and the actors' charter is complete. Again, the loyalty is currently little noted; but the taking it for granted, both by actors and audience, may be the best compliment that either could pay it. The actors of the chief parts have the play's fortunes in their hands, each other's fortunes too; and the actors of the least conspicuous parts, by the slightest lapse from loyalty, can do it disproportionate damage. Seldom or never is there any such lapse. They all combine to build a structure of mutual understanding and trust. And it is to more than play-acting, I repeat, that these principles of play-acting can be made to apply.

THE CASTING OF A PLAY:
AMONG ACTORS; AMONG STUDENTS

Classwork, we said, which is in its nature cooperative, suits the cooperative nature of the drama well. And, in studying a play it will obviously be convenient, at some time, to distribute its parts among the students very much as they are cast among a company of actors. But not wholly: the difference of aim—for the student no performance being in prospect—will demand a readjustment of method in more than one respect. It may be better not to give a student such entire possession of a part as an actor is given. For one reason, proprietary care of it may weaken his interest in the play as a whole; for another, if it is a very small part, he may be wearied of it before the play as a whole can have been fully studied. A simple and obvious plan with plays of such a multitude of characters as have *Antony and Cleopatra* or *Peer Gynt* would be to allot the longer parts singly and the shorter ones in bunches, or to ring the changes on them among the less advanced students. But there is something to be said—our purpose being pure study—for ridding the student altogether of this sense of property in a part, big or small. It is a moot point; and it raises the whole question of adapting the classwork to a variety of methods of study.

There will remain the capital difference (already noted) between the actor's self-surrender, pending from the start, and the student's sustained detachment. Yet (also noted) this latter is to be no mere bookish understanding of the play but a lively appreciation of it too; and there can be more than one way of gaining that. It will depend on the disposition of the student. To one the analytical approach will be easy. Trait by trait he will uncover and be ready to defend to the rest of the class, the character of his Hamlet, Oedipus or John Gabriel Borkman. Another student may go to work in quite another way—but one equally, and even more legitimate —trying first to identify himself imaginatively with the character, then proceeding by argument to justify his intuition. It can be called more legitimate since we are committed to study of our art as nearly as possible in its own terms, and by this method the student at the outset exposes the sensitive plate of his mind to the impression the play makes on it, very much as does the audience to its performance—which for enjoyment suffices the audience. Such a student, incidentally, may protest that having to put his deeply felt appreciation into words—mere words!—will only coarsen it. But his class fellows will have their right to argument, analysis and explanation. They are not to be content, for instance, with his assurance that he inwardly knows just how Macbeth feels at that moment. And can't they tell this by the way he speaks the lines? Then he'll speak them again. And he does so ad libitum, and we are no further on. So to reconcile the diversely gifted students, the quick in perception but weak in argument with the logically minded, I should be disposed, were I conducting such a class, to put parts which invited much discussion into commission, as it were. I would sooner have, not one Hamlet or one Iago, but three; as the old rhyme runs "One to watch and one to pray, and one to keep the Devil away." And the Devil in this case can safely be identified with the spirit sure to enter into some student in such a class, convincing him that Macbeth is Bothwell or Hamlet a portrait of the Earl of Essex, Claudius of Leicester, Gertrude of Queen Elizabeth and Ophelia of the Dark Lady of the Sonnets; any excuse for talking such nonsense seeming sometimes to be better than none, with the best part of the hour wasted in escaping from the silly tangle. Let us note therefore in passing that the work of the class, since it is not to reach the solidity of action, should be only the more securely anchored to common sense.* A play is in

* There would need to be also, I think, a running record kept of

its nature a business of make-believe; and one degree of make-believe—a single thickness of fiction—is all that it will effectively carry.

To this point of likeness, then, and with this main difference, should we cast a play for study as for stage. For certain complex characters, to be given to certain sorts of student, better the convinced advocate than the would-be actor, who will only feel baffled when he is stopped short of acting. I should be anxious too—were I conducting such a class—to leave the less histrionically equipped students at no disadvantage.

THE EXPLICIT AND IMPLICIT METHODS OF PLAYWRITING

Take next the question of more and less suitable material for our study. There are roughly—considering both

the progress of the class. Some sub-professor or super-student should at short intervals summarize the work done and the consensus of opinion reached (reservations noted) upon the more important issues that have come up for discussion: e.g. how much knowledge or suspicion has Gertrude of Claudius' guilt, and how much of this should —or can—the actress show? Is Lady Macbeth's swoon upon Macbeth's too glib account of his killing of the grooms who are to be saddled with the murder of Duncan, genuine or a trick to take attention from him? What are we meant to gather in *Rosmersholm* of Rebecca West's relations to the dead Dr. West—and what do we gather? It should be a business-like record, not aspiring to any literary style. It should primarily aim at reminding the class continually of the play's purport, and at keeping us conscious of its form. For this finds expression mainly in its action; and our restraint from that will leave us the more dangerously free to talk at large, saying, no doubt, many smart and illuminating things about the play, but not identifying ourselves with it closely enough. Authors of every sort are subject to the weakness, which lets them set out to write about one thing and go on writing about another. It is a weakness that the discipline of the dramatic form helps correct. And equally in merely studying a play it is as well to keep on the narrow track.

[43]

today's and yesterday's—two methods of playwriting, that demanding explicit interpretation, and that in which much of the meaning is left implicit, to be conveyed by the actors, not in words nor even in very forthright action, but largely by demonstrating the sort of pattern made in the relations and attitude of the characters toward each other and in the contrasts between them, the dialogue stressing the significance of the design thus formed. Marlowe's, for an example, is wholly "explicit" drama, as is more primitive drama than his. So are Shakespeare's earlier plays, and his method in general remains throughout as explicit as the nature of play or character will allow it to be. Chekov's method, on the other hand, and sometimes Maeterlinck's or Yeats', are "implicit" in the extreme. Yet it is not a difference between modern drama and old. No dramatist could be more explicit than is Bernard Shaw, and others have been returning lately to old forms, while not half the significance in *King Lear* and *Macbeth* finds its way into plain words. But, speaking generally, it is the increased use of the implicit in drama which has marked its more modern developments ("modern" for me, I fear, meaning Ibsen and Chekov and Maeterlinck; my junior listeners must apply some other epithet), and the demands made on the actors have so far developed as to have almost completely changed. Romeo and Juliet, for instance, can be acted by a couple of children if they can speak and move as aptly as well-trained choir boys can sing (Shakespeare's Juliet, of course, was so acted, and nobody now thinks of commiserating him upon that; I have even heard him envied). So, indeed, can such a partly and comparatively "implicit" a play as Macbeth be. In default of great acting for it, simple acting will be the next best thing; impersonal, plastically pleasing, showing as much regard as possible for Shakespeare's share in the business and as little for the actors' own. The tragedy will still yield us much, and its better part. But in Chekov's The Cherry Orchard, unless the actress of Madame Ranevsky brings to her performance not only all she is directed to say and do, but something besides that it is suggested she must pervasively and expressively be (and the same thing will be true and truer of acting in the later plays of that both explicit and implicit dramatist Ibsen) there will be left in the place the character should fill nothing but a very large hole. In most sorts of drama the actor's personality, animating and clothing the figure the dramatist has designed, will be a legitimate factor (if only, as we said, the distinction can be kept between personality manifested and ego exploited) ; in this implicit sort it is positively needed, the art of the dramatist providing for and demanding it. And this, in turn, calls on all that is maturest in the art of the actor. He may spend a professional lifetime making himself into an instrument that, for the dramatist's benefit, he can so sensitively play upon.

Little or nothing is to be gained from fully filled-in student performances of this implicit drama, from a Rebecca West or Hedda Gabler acted by—to put it unkindly, as we should at first glance—precocious schoolgirls, or from a Master Builder listening for the younger generation knocking at the door played by one of that very generation, vaultingly ambitious. On the other hand, the student, remaining a student, nor trying to reach to more than the fullest intellectual and emotional appreciation of it of which he is capable, will be less at a disadvantage with this sort of play, however inadequate his powers of *expression* may be; since—whether for student or actor—there is the more work to be done at it before putting it into action, and that dividing line can therefore be drawn the later. Our class can, in fact, very profitably *study* a play which they could not hope to *perform* with much benefit to themselves or pleasure to anybody else.

THE COOPERATIVE TASK

Their first step in their cooperative task will be to come to a common understanding of the play, complete enough, at any rate, to be "workable." Of what we are to mean by workable take this example. Hedda Gabler kills herself. There may be much difference of opinion in the class—most importantly between the two or three students who have been appointed "counsel" for Hedda —as to precisely why she did so; still, as long as it is accepted that she would have done so, the incident remains workable. But Judge Brack, it will be remembered, that apostle of the polite conventions, cries out when the fatal shot is heard. "God help us: people don't *do* these things." And if we think—to put it so—that the play he might have written about her (the play which he was so ready to act out in life), with its happy ending in adultery, would have been the likelier one, why, there is plainly an *unworkable* difference of opinion between us and Ibsen himself. Then we must either begin to study her again or condemn the dramatist for inconsistency and weakness for a startling "curtain." And that, I remind you, we are, as students, quite at liberty to do, indeed, honestly bound to do; although as actors, set to perform the play, and about to identify ourselves with the characters, we soon should not be.

Then, a common understanding must be reached as to the main lines of the action of the play. Even though our students are not to put it into action they must still imagine this rightly done. With the average play of today or yesterday, written for a familiar form of theater, few questions, it may be said, can arise on this score, since the dramatist will usually have made plain—and we shall readily understand—what he wants done. But when a play was written for a theater which is now unfamiliar— as Sheridan's is somewhat, Molière's rather more, Shakespeare's much more, the Greek theater wholly—and when moreover, as will then generally be the case, its action must be deduced from the framework of its speech, which was all the dramatist considered needed writing down for his interpreters at the time; why, this leaves room for conjecture, and discussion is needed. The movements of the chorus in the *Agamemnon*, supplementing those of the characters on the stage, the marching and countermarching of the armies in *Antony and Cleopatra* and *Coriolanus*, these, and other such combinations of structure and action, are integral parts of the play. And, studying it, since we are not to see them, we must keep them only the more vividly in our mind's eye, or they will continually tend to fall back again and be reabsorbed in that sparsely printed page from which our imagination has had to evoke them.

The structure of the "explicit" play—its action so clearly supplementing its speech, its speech explaining its action—cannot be hard to discern. Its qualities will lie in a well told story worth telling, in a balancing of interests and the contrasting of the characters; for the rest, in such poetic rhetoric, it may be, as Hotspur's, in Falstaff's robust or Rosalind's lively prose, or in that of Eliot's chastened writing or of Shaw's masterly eloquence. The worth or shortcomings of the storytelling, its balances and contrasts, ask no special knowledge for their demonstrating. The proof of such speech doubtless lies best in its speaking; and this can be a troublesomely expert business. The essentials of the art are, as we said, properly to be learnt at an earlier than college age. But, granted some equipment in them, the student will often be able to bring to the "explicit" play's demands in this kind a freshness of response which the over-practiced actor may have lost. And if he does not, even should he be able to exhibit at this stage no more than a token value of (say) Hotspur's spirited defense of the withholding of the prisoners, or the Inquisitor's speech in Shaw's *Joan of Arc*, so long as it is enough for evidence that he appreciates their quality, the educational loss will not be great.

THE STUDY OF A PLAY PUTS IT
ON TRIAL

The classwork by which the students will test and augment their own knowledge necessarily becomes also something like a test and trial of the play. We consider it first as a whole. Though it may seldom be planned in any strict obedience to the famous Unities, some sort of unity it must have. An approximate unity of subject will be convenient, if the attention of an audience is to be happily held, and a unity of convention, for the sustaining of the make-believe. But the conditions of the theater positively force on the drama certain limiting disciplines. The actors—for a dominating instance—are physically limited in what they can do; and this human medium affects all that touches it. The dramatist, then, will not employ his scenic conventions in a fashion which they, the actors, cannot make convincing. Shakespeare inherits in his theater, with its platform stage and illocalized balconies and curtains, a seemingly untrammelled freedom in space and time, and his audience would yield to his suggestions a most obedient imagination. But, with his extraordinary sense of the theater, he never taxes this aimlessly or too far, never leaves us questioning. Convention in the theater is a gentleman's agreement between dramatist, actors, and audience. It involves (as do all agreements) consistency, and consideration in the use of it. Shakespeare retains the scenic freedoms of his bare stage, but he uses them considerately. Ibsen, writing for his theater of scenic illusion, has surrendered them, has, so to put it, anchored himself in space, and, more closely

[49]

than any of his predecessors, in time. And he cannot arbitrarily resume his freedom. He makes a half-attempt to do so in his last two plays, when John Gabriel Borkman sets off up the snow-bound mountain, in the ending of *When We Dead Awaken* amid avalanches and hymns to freedom. But this does not quite do. The agreement has been broken. The actors may not object; but we, the audience, having first accepted one sort of illusion, will be unwilling suddenly to change; and against our discomfort neither dramatist nor actors can successfully contend. Audience and actors must be at ease together.*

* It may be argued that an audience having seen a play given on one night under conditions of scenic illusion will accept without difficulty Shakespeare and his conventions the next. Yes; but until how recently has Shakespeare not been adapted to the conventions of the contemporary stage? To a degree he still is. To a degree it is because this is "Shakespeare" that an intimidated audience will swallow his stagecraft (nearly) whole. There have lately been, it may be added, various experiments in convention. But they have remained experiments, no general change has developed from them; not, certainly, from one pseudo-Chinese production I remember, nor from a most delightful one out of two projected by Mr. Thornton Wilder. And I doubt whether, in any of the three instances, the parties to the business—author, actors and audience—were wholly at their ease. A certain self-consciousness, an air of artificial innocence, pervaded it.

Of more importance is Mr. T. S. Eliot's recent *The Family Reunion*, with its modern treatment of the matter of a Greek tragedy. The conventions are mixed: but the actual inclusion of the Eumenides among the characters—mute, but visible both to hero and audience—is for me at once the unlikeliest and the least necessary of the devices. Mr. Eliot has not yet mastered, I think, with perfect certainty the visually imaginative side of his dramatic art. On the other hand, the treatment of chorus and dialogue, the significant blending of realistic and formal, I find masterly indeed. And while it would be work, truly, for very advanced students, in a testing trial of this play, a distinguishing between its achievements and its shortcomings, we should be dealing with some of the fundamentals of drama.

[50]

THE QUESTION OF DRAMATIC INTEGRITY

More vital, however, than consistency of convention will be the inner quality of dramatic integrity. A play, as we said, involves conflict, outward or inward; this keeps it alive. Its story will be told chiefly by the setting out of differences between the characters. The action develops these and will dispose of them, be it, as in comedy, by reconciliation and agreement or by tragic catastrophe— and there are variations enough between the two extremes. The point is that the differences must always be fairly fought out, each character being allowed to say and do his best on his own behalf. There must be no fraudulent tipping of the scales by the dramatist in favor of this one or that, no lucky, but too unlikely accident occurring, no over-opportune conversions from one opinion to another. For the fraud of these will be at once detected, unless the audience is as gullible as the dramatist is dishonest. And characters so indulged will at once lose their dramatic integrity. They will forfeit their seemingly independent status in that mimic world which we have agreed to accept for an hour or so as the real world. At the sign of such weakness, such a lapse into puppetdom, we in turn shall weaken in our belief in it, and in them. And it is by this belief—willingly accorded at first, yet to be lost all but unawares—that the maturer art of the drama subsists.

Very much as we feel that a man may be called on to justify his existence in the real world, so must a character's place, speech and actions in such a play, be justifiable. And the student temporarily identifying himself

with a character or given its interests to defend, will have
to make a case for them against whatever devil's advocacy
the rest of the class can muster. The brief, on the face
of it, may seem but a meager one. What the character
does and says, what is said *to* the character, what *about* it
—in strictness that can be all; and except possibly for
certain forms of poetry there can be no thriftier kind of
writing than the dramatic. A stock curiosity in my youth
was the Lord's Prayer written on a threepenny piece. In
such a script the whole of Lady Macbeth could, I suppose, be accommodated on a silver dollar, and Hamlet—
the part if not the play—on the front and back of a dollar
bill. And Shakespeare's was a comparatively verbose
school of writing ("explicit" we have called it) delighting
in words and their beauty. He had, moreover, to suggest
in words such scenery as he might think the play needed,
a background for its action; and in every play space and
time must be spared in which to tell the audience all that
needs to be known of what has happened before the action begins, in providing it, so to say, with the background
of its past. There are simple ways of building up this past,
be it of the play as a whole or of a single character; by the
Prologue bringing the story to the point at which the
action begins and can, in the present tense, and unencum-
bered, carry it on; by narrative embodied in the action,
shaped, perhaps, as reminiscences exchanged between the
characters. Familiar devices range from *Romeo and
Juliet's* "Two houses both alike in dignity . . ." to the
opening of almost any nineteenth century French farce
with its valet and chambermaid, and their "Didn't Mas-

ter get home very late last night? . . ."* But the student will find that, as the art of the drama matures, his brief on behalf of a character is reduced to the dimensions and the stuff of the character itself.

IBSEN AND HIS "ROSMERSHOLM"

Turn to Ibsen, that artist and craftsman combined; not the Ibsen of the history plays, nor of *Brand* and *Peer Gynt*, but the Ibsen who protests he has forsworn the poetic drama, though in truth he had only found out how to write it in prose. His technical aim now is to make his play's action and his characters as self-explanatory as possible; and what needs to be known of the past will be brought out in terms of its interest to the present. For the present tense is the dramatic tense. A play's dialogue is a species of conflict, sportive or bitter, usually a series of duels varied by more general fighting. The mere looking backwards of narrative or reminiscence will soon slacken our interest; it is at best as if the combatants were resting between bouts to exchange memories of past fighting. Ibsen aims also at giving his characters that seeming independence of the author, of which we spoke, for an attribute to their dramatic integrity; and to do this he sacrifices the convenient and time-honored

* For the classic burlesque of this method see, of course, Sheridan's *The Critic*; Sir Walter Raleigh to Sir Christopher Hatton: "You know, my friend, scarce two revolving suns. . . . You know, besides. . . . You also know . . ." and so on, until Dangle interrupts with "But, Mr. Puff, as he knows all this, why does Sir Walter go on telling him?" to be snubbed by a "But the audience are not supposed to know anything of the matter, are they?" Not such sheer burlesque, either!

devices of the aside and soliloquy, by which their intimate thought and feelings could be directly revealed to the audience. Shakespeare's stage had few scenic furnishings; Ibsen in turn strips his of all such conventions as these. So little is there in his dialogue to remind us of the theater that we seem less to be *hearing* these conversations from our stalls than privately over-hearing them.

Yet this talk, which will seem not meant for our ears, is to be made to bring us into as close a touch with *Rosmersholm's* Rebecca West as his soliloquies, all but addressed to us, bring Hamlet; the very souls of the Rita and Alfred Allmers of *Little Eyolf* are to be laid bare to us, and to themselves. Here is the paradox of great drama. This most material of the arts becomes, in the hands of its masters, one of the choicest vehicles for inward revelation, and, thanks to the familiarity of its human medium, the most convincing. Ibsen's problem in plays of the *Rosmersholm* technique is, while keeping the talk just such as the immediate occasion would produce, to fill it besides with all else that the play's working out demands; and every passage of the dialogue is put to double—sometimes, indeed, to triple—use. It must advance the actual action, revealing the character of the speakers as it does so. It may show us the character of the listeners also, by their mute response—or lack of response —to it. And bit by bit—the delays increasing our suspense, —the story of the past comes out, of Rebecca's crime, of how ruthlessly she lured the unhappy Beata to suicide, so that, she told herself, Rosmer might be spiritually free. And this builds up the never-seen Beata's character too.

Further, into the unornamented talk and the few simple
comings and goings of the action—Rosmer's slow, haunted
movements, Rebecca's quiet tread, Madam Helseth's
pleasant homeliness for contrast—there is woven a picture
of Rosmersholm itself. Not descriptively, in competition
with scene-painting and carpentry; we have the atmos-
phere of the old house, in which children neither laugh
nor cry (says Madam Helseth), with its traditions of
conformity and order, its mill-race thundering without,
and the legend of the White Horses. Time is even found
for a few words about the pugnacious Rector Kroll's
domestic troubles, for a glimpse into Mortensgård's scan-
dal-dogged past, for twin flashes across the scene of the
tragi-comic idealist Ulric Brendel; and these strokes of a
picture of what is happening *around* Rosmersholm, re-
flected from what is happening *within* Rosmersholm,
make this the more vivid.

For it all contributes to the main action of the play,
which is the spiritual tragedy of Rosmer and Rebecca,
with its discoveries and disclosures and their consequences. Rebecca has learnt of herself, since she began
to gather in the harvest of her ill-doing, that her motives
for it were not so noble as she liked to think; of Rosmer
she learns that he is not the man to profit by freedom
even ignorantly so gained. He discovers that he loves her
and has always loved her. But it is with a love that has
transformed—*she* discovers—her passion for him into a
like love which will not let her profit by her sin. And
instead of freeing his mind from its trammels she has only
taught him to despair, while he has taught her to take

the "Rosmersholm" view of life, which demands atonement for sin. Finally, to be free of this wreck of their beliefs, the tangle of doubt, the intolerable strain, they go to their death together by the way the wronged Beata went. And the old servant cries out as she sees it, "The dead wife has taken them!"

That is a poor enough epitome of the two hours of overheard talk (itself a masterpiece of condensation) which is the total matter of the play. His usual two years of brooding work went to its writing; and our class could, I think, give it a fair number of hours of study without milking it dry of interest, technical and metaphysical too. There are only six characters, and two of them have no more than a passing concern with the story; but two at least—Rebecca most certainly—are many-faceted enough in their showing to invite more than one approach, provide for ample discussion; and their dramatic integrity will stand the test of the closest analysis. Rosmersholm, moreover, is the kind of play (there are not many of its kind and quality combined, by Ibsen or anybody else!) which can be made to yield the most to sheer study, in which the lack of the action, so little is there, will leave the least lacking. And in that it will meet our class's demands.

But it is an exciting play too. It is a spiritual detective story. The facts of Rebecca's crime come out easily enough; and they are all that would have interested the commonplace dramatist, or would appeal, supposedly, to a commonplace audience.* More interesting are the mo-

* There was, indeed, in London at the time of the play's first pro-

tives; that is true of any crime. And it is out of the complex of these, gradually disentangled and revealed, that
the pattern of the past—of the derivative action, so to call
it—is assembled for us. But more interesting yet are the
accumulating consequences of these revelations to the
human souls concerned. The play's actual action—its
present tense—is in these. It throws a light into the very
depths of man's nature and upon some of the mysteries
that lie there.

Ibsen draws no moral. Even as for the telling of the
story and the unfolding of character he has discarded
soliloquy, aside, and every other such open acknowledg-
ment of his audience, so now—all said and done that need
be—he brings the play to an uncommented end.* For the
dramatist's business is not to moralize, but simply to see
that—as to a question asked—his play tells the truth in
reply, and that it is a significant truth, worth the telling.
Our business is to cultivate—to sharpen and refine—
our hearing and appreciation until we can swiftly distinguish between what is significant and truly told, and what

duction there, a gentleman who wrote under the name of Austin
Fryers, and who—contending that Ibsen had missed the true point
of his own work—perpetrated a sort of prologue to it, which he
called Beata, in which he dealt with her side of the story, setting
out in three—doubtless very lively—acts the matter which the dun-
derheaded Norwegian had compressed into four or five reminiscent
speeches, for use merely as the seed of his tragedy of character.

* The precisian may object that Madam Helseth's closing out-
burst is both comment and soliloquy. The answer to this can be that
under great stress of emotion people do so exclaim out loud, to themselves, and sometimes in turned sentences too. If that is not accept-
able let us say that Ibsen was too experienced a dramatist not to
know when he could advantageously break his own rules.

oftenest, in a poor play, is neither. And—yet once more —this is a very educative exercise.

BUT STUDY LEAVES THE PLAY, AS IT FINDS IT, A WORK OF ART

The "overheard" play such as Rosmersholm—with its compact story asking all attention and its complex of emotions painfully unravelling—offers much to the student even in demanding much from him, and more than a lesson in stagecraft. For the art of the dramatist presents it very nearly as the matter of it might happen in life; and such self-identifying study of it as we have in mind will all but measure up to an experience vicariously undergone. And from this our student may emerge, if not a little wiser than he was—wisdom comes more slowly—at least a little keener in discerning the things about him. Rebecca's case, it may be said, is not a common one. There will not, it is fairly certain, be any young woman listening to me with a Beata for a rival, as anxious to get rid of her—and with a mill-stream handy too! Yet one never knows. As Grant Allen said when the critics of fifty years ago cried out on Hedda Gabler as a quite impossible character, "Nonsense; I take her down to dinner once a week." There will not be in my audience many young men whose uncles have murdered their fathers and debauched their mothers, but there will be few who have not found themselves faced at some time, in one form or another, with some of Hamlet's moral problems. To which point I will return later.

Finally, we must not let our study of a play discount

its value to us as a work of art. We pull it to pieces for educational use very much as actors do in rehearsing it, but with this chief difference, that we do not have to consider putting it together again, as they must, for the performance which will complete and justify its existence. Our students will not possess the special skill for that or be equipped to acquire it; nor, then, will they wisely wish to exchange the student's critical for the actor's devoted attitude. And, having well studied a play, they really should have gained too much regard for it to be ready to defame it by a crude performance. But such students will make the best possible audience for the best possible performance of it that can be given. And they will have earned the right to this. How it might be provided for them is another question.

III

A Theater That Might Be

PATRONAGE AND CENSORSHIP

WE spoke, in passing, of the effects of patronage upon the various British arts. Upon that of the drama they have been peculiar. It was, so to say, bred, if not born, in patronage. The early companies of actors were known as the King's Men, the Queen's, the Lord Chamberlain's, the Lord Admiral's Men; and without some such badge of protection they could not follow their calling, but were liable to arrest as "rogues and vagabonds."* For those were still the days in England when a man had to "belong" somewhere, to be a recognized part of the body politic. When the Puritans came into power both plays and players were summarily suppressed; and, when the King's restoration permitted theirs, it was, as with other things, under less feudal conditions. The sovereign, through the Lord Chamberlain, had the customary power of licensing or disallowing all dramatic performances; and Charles II now gave "patents" to two of his courtiers, privileging them to muster two companies and build two theaters. And he gave each of them besides the exclusive rights to a long list of plays—Shakespeare's were divided between them—which, by our modern notions of property, were not his to give. But it was effective patronage—as far as it went. And it went

* I believe this to be the only application of that much quoted phrase.

[61]

thus much further, that he was himself an assiduous playgoer. I only hope he paid for his seats (I do not know; there is a point in theatrical history, which it behooves some student to investigate). That, at any rate, was as far as it did go. And ever since "patronage" of the theater, whether by kings or lesser folk, has commonly meant this and little more.*

The power of the royal prerogative has by now diminished to a shadow, except in the matter of the licensing of plays; and there it is still solid enough, though it may be more timidly handled than it once was. But within my own recollection it proved a mischievous clog upon what looked to be a very promising renaissance of the English theater. The positive harm done may not have seemed great, the forbidding the public stage to a dozen plays or so: *The Cenci, Ghosts, Monna Vanna, Mrs. Warren's Profession, Les Avariés, La Citta Morta*, and some by lesser men. There was no "money" in any of them, nor the making of a procession or a riot or a Trafalgar Square meeting as a protest against their suppression. I remember the Home Secretary of that day telling me privately that if we organized a protest of sufficient violence to make the Government thoroughly uncomfortable—why,

* Readers of *Nicholas Nickleby* will remember Miss Snevellicci's bespeak, Mr. Curdle on the unities of the drama, and the three half-crowns. "And," said Miss Snevellicci, "I assure you . . . that I think myself very lucky they did not owe all the money instead of being sixpence short. Now, if you were to succeed, they would give people to understand that they had always patronized you; and if you were to fail, they would have been quite certain of that from the very beginning." But there has been generous patronage of the drama in England as well as mean, generous and extravagant; little that has been both generous and wise.

something might be done. But otherwise, to expect a cabinet of Liberal Ministers to add such a trifle as this, quite gratuitously, to their many weightier troubles, showed, on my part, a regrettable political innocence. Did I, in particular, at a time when Home Rule, a "People's Budget" and the Parliament Act were looming, expect them to lay a finger upon one of the few remaining —and politically quite harmless—odds and ends of royal authority? But to this day the Lord Chamberlain's powers over the theater are little less despotic than they were in Queen Elizabeth's reign. They are at one with other time-worn traditions that the English lovingly cling to—the Woolsack, the ceremonies in Parliament, the state coach with its eight cream-colored ponies, the Beefeaters, and the rest of the trappings. I cling to them myself when the price to be paid in realities is not too high. But here it is so; for drama is something more than an amusing pageant. And the price paid has been not less than the degradation of its entire status. The drama has been compulsorily patronized; but with this has gone no obligation on the part of the patron to support it. In other countries, kings and the governments that replaced them assumed one. The theater became a recognized public institution. See how the French people, with France at her poorest, would receive a proposal to abolish the *Comédie Française*. A few years ago an act of gross contempt for its administration was worth a very black mark indeed against the Minister responsible. But in England and— originally by example—in this country too its status is merely commercial.

Now, by that it has in the past earned a certain respect, the respect which a self-supporting industry can always claim, on this ground if no other. And, during these latter years, treaty-making with cinema and radio has brought much extra prosperity to actor, director and dramatist according to the popularity they have achieved; and to the financiers, the money-spinners who exploit them, probably even more. It is idle to condemn success; nor need one as long as it is clear under what conditions the success is gained and what the sequel is likely to be. Well, more and more it looks as if the drama, properly so called, were forfeiting its independence, losing its peculiar quality, and might sink into place as one of the pettier parts of a gigantic entertainment industry, to the demands of which it must obediently adapt itself. It is at present bargaining for its livelihood. It still has prestige to sell, which is mostly associated with the personality of a few favorite actors and actresses; but the competitive value of even this is, I fear, diminishing. And I do not think that a summary of the fortunes—and misfortunes—of the New York theater, which I happened to see in some newspaper and note at the finish of its last season, is evidence to the contrary. This records the staging of seventy-three plays and more. A "success" may have registered some two thousand consecutive performances. A so-called failure will have been shoved out of the way as quickly as possible; its losses cut. A play is said to do good or bad "business"; it makes or loses money, that is to say; and there is no other yardstick of success and failure. But is this popular verdict—probably to be given, moreover, at the pistol's point of a weekly tenancy of a theater—a really satisfactory measure of the quality of a play?

A conspicuous place in the record falls to the two million and a half dollars worth of "screen sales" made. A satisfactory item, no doubt, to those that pocket the money, but of a very indirect benefit to the drama. A detailed balance sheet of the financing of the New York theater industry, closely analyzed, would, I imagine, be an illuminating document. But we should see a picture, I suppose, of what a conservatively minded banker or lawyer might possibly consider financial disorder—out of which, nevertheless, a skillful operator in this market, careful to keep hold of the thick end of the stick (that being the ownership of those strange and uncomfortable buildings in which plays are performed) will manage to fish a steady little profit year by year. The sponsors of the plays themselves gamble more headily. As to the actors and directors, while the sun of a "success" shines, they make all the hay they can; when it stops shining they must be ready to pack up quick and seek better weather elsewhere. It may be, of course, that this queer combination of usury and gambling, this general irresponsibility, suits the drama well enough, since it is, in some aspects, the most volatile and ephemeral of the arts. Is not perhaps the true spirit of it best fostered in happy-go-lucky, shiftless levity? Thespis and his cart, Hogarth's strolling players in their barn, Mr. Vincent Crummles and the Infant Phenomenon—there was a lot of fun in them; and every now and then an Edmund Kean would come tramping through the mud. But, alas, the simplicity and innocence of this seem gone beyond recall; and there is something incongruously vulgar about a bank account in Bohemia.

WHAT IS A THEATER?

The four hundred year history of the English-speaking theater shows one or two short periods in which companies of actors working loyally together did their calling some credit, and a number of notable individual careers. For the rest, it is a record of episode after episode, all to a pattern; of passing triumphs, and disasters soon forgotten, storms in teacups, vanities displayed and tempers lost, much dull daily work honestly done and ignored, much ploughing of the sands. But it is ill belaboring the people of the theater for their human frailties, which differ most from those of other people in being easier to advertise. What history must ask of any theater is chiefly this: has it, throughout the years, done well and worthily by the drama given into its charge?

In view of its difficulties, "Not so badly," is, I suppose, a fair answer. True, we have no House of Shakespeare, as the French have their House of Molière, which is besides, of course, a home—if a not too accommodating one—for Corneille, Racine, Victor Hugo, Rostand, Becque, some of whose work at least it is charged to keep alive (incidentally it has become of late years a Parisian piéd-à-terre for Shakespeare). We English-speaking peoples have a drama—a four hundred year

[66]

accumulation of it—outranked by none in the world. And, thanks to recurring spells of enthusiasm, backed often by preposterous self-sacrifice, it has so far managed to rally time and again, even from its worst doldrums. But we have no such theater. Why not? In England the truthfulest answer to this as to similar questions would simply be: because we never have had. But that is no answer here in the United States; the best of reasons, rather, for having one if other reasons are good. No such theater! And, it can be added, nothing in any English-speaking country that is properly to be called a theater at all. A man I knew long ago had passed the most energetic years of his life both creditably and successfully in various theatrical pursuits; and he suddenly vanished from those scenes. I asked him when I met him some time later, "Why did you leave the theater?" He answered me, "Because there was none to leave."

By "theater" he evidently did not mean, then, merely one of those buildings in which a scratch company of actors can be assembled and a play rehearsed and performed time after time to a casual crowd at so much a head until the immediate demand for it is exhausted. For a true theater a building is needed, certainly, even as is a factory for the manufacturing of motorcars or fountain pens, and the better equipped the factory the more efficient and economical the manufacture will be. But by a theater (he explained) he meant rather, and before all, a stable organization of actors and actresses and directors, an institution in which the whole art of the drama can be cultivated for its own sake and made manifest.

There would be performances, of course; an audience is a necessary sounding-board for a play. And this audience had better as a matter of form be let pay something for their seats; they will—such is human nature—value them the more, and so not conduct themselves toward the institution too casually. And the numbers in which they came to contrasted plays would be a current and helpful test of the relations between the theater and its public. For those must be kept healthy and friendly; no institution can properly exist to itself alone. But plays would no more be performed in such a theater for the *sole* purpose of attracting a crowd than a Flemish primitive will be bought or rejected by the Metropolitan Museum upon the taking of a city-wide plebiscite (the time may come when the public taste will be so reliable, but it has not come yet), or than New York's public librarian will timidly fill his shelves with nothing but best-sellers.

The parallel between such a theater and museum or library cannot be exact since their economy differs so widely. A picture may be put on pretty permanent exhibition, a play cannot be; and while a single reader can be allowed to take from its shelf a book that he wants, the manager of the theater must feel convinced that a certain number of people will be attracted by the play (even if patience be needed) before he sets in motion the somewhat complex machinery for putting it on the stage. But the relation of all three institutions to the public, and the services that those working in them may render to the fine arts and literature and drama, will in essence be very much the same. A good library will aim at stocking its shelves with as many as may be of the representative books of the world, a good picture gallery at possessing representative specimens of painting. Does the library, incidentally, compete unfairly, or at all, with the bookseller? No; it encourages people to read and even buy books they might never choose for themselves. Indirectly, picture galleries sell pictures to those who there learn to like them. Music needs foresighted organization and endowment, so by now it seems to be agreed, if we are to have other than catchpenny music. The drama depends more upon organization than does any other art. Is it to be the only one left wholly to the higgling of the market?

If a graph could be drawn of the fortunes of the theater in England it is the first fifty years or so of its history that would show the sharpest ascent. Then comes the Puritan break; after its mending, fortuitous ups and downs, periods of credit and of more or less discredit. Already, at the end of the seventeenth century, the author of *Historia Histrionica* is lamenting the good old days of the King's Company, headed by those "grave and sober men, living in reputation." Later come Garrick, the Kembles, Macready, Irving, Booth; brilliant, and of their sort, imposing figures. But they and the rest all pass, leaving only memories behind them. This has been counted an inevitable limitation of the actor's art; those belittling it kindly allowing the extravagant applause it sometimes earns to be but fair compensation for the unkindness. Is the future to be otherwise? The last few years with their inventions have raised the question. Are the screen and the record to combine henceforth to confer a sort of mechanical immortality upon the actor?

THE MOVIE

These inventions—it is possible—are as yet in their infancy only. Science even now offers us, for the turning of a switch, the voice of a singer, the sound of an orchestra—and whether it is the voice of the dead or the living, whether the music is being made now while we listen or was recorded years ago, who is to tell? Every movie we see and hear, however new, is a record of the past; whether it was taken a month or ten years back will soon make little difference. And we are promised a perfecting of television, which will certainly be susceptible of record too; so that a man may sit at home before his own silver screen and switch on the picture of his choice; not merely the latest thing, but, if he is in the mood, that which once charmed him, when the stars that shone in it shone more refulgently than they could do today (wisely retired upon their savings, he will trust). And except for the relief simply of going out and getting away from home—an important factor, however, this!— here is one likely prospect for the great entertainment industry. Its products will be brought to our doors with the milk and the groceries. And if the traditional, old-fashioned, drama comes to selling itself yet more extensively for a well-paid petty share in that, it can look, of course, to a similar prospect. And why should it not? Why put up these cumbrous and costly buildings and mobilize actors in them night after night to parrot a play through, when science will enable us, after taking all the pains needed to prepare the best performances possible— a single one sufficing—to record it and preserve it? As it is, the finest performances of the greatest plays are con- demned to share the human mortality of the actors that animate them. The marvelous movie has shown us, surely, a better way. Let us have done with the theater as we now know it and set to work accumulating libraries of records of the drama. The art of Titian, of Verrocchio, of Beethoven is preserved to us. Already the great musicians of today are more widely known by records than in per- son. Why should not the future Garrick or Kean be given just such immortality?

It sounds the right sort of thing for a scientific age. What would be wrong with it? I want to absolve myself from any suspicion of prejudice against the movie. I have never been concerned in making one; but I am a con- firmed movie-goer, and have been from the days of its restful silence (but for the buzzing of the projector and the anomalous clatter of the piano), the tentative days when movie-makers took plays for their models very much as the earliest railroad builders made trains of horse-carriages fastened on trucks. Since then they have found their own formulas, and the technical advance has been amazing. The movie can, of course, do things that the theater can never compass, and it is seen at its best, possibly, in doing them. The best movie-makers, I should suppose, think and plan chiefly in terms of pictures from the beginning. What is there, if anything, that the old- fashioned theater can do and the movie cannot? And here, you may say, I am bound to be prejudiced. I learnt to enjoy the theater before the movie was born. The millions who now learn to enjoy the movie before ever they see a play acted—if they ever do—may equally be disappointed by the cramping conventions of the theater. There is no absolute standard in such matters, and I do not attempt to dictate one. I can but note the effect made on me and do my best to explain it.

I find that what I look for and like best in the movie is technical achievement; striking photography will do much to atone for the banality of the scenes photographed. But pleasure in spectacle is quickly gratified, and less readily renewable. One seldom wants to see a movie twice. And the movie-maker seems to be forever trying to reconcile his public's craze for novelty with the financial safety of the accustomed thing. But a craze for novelty will be the curse of any art. Now spectacle plays a small part in the theater, for more than a modicum of it can only depreciate the actor's share in a play. And it is in the actor and his acting that the pulse of the drama beats. If the movie, then, is to make the drama its own, it must do as well by the actor as the theater has done. So far, of course, it has not; and to deny this is merely to show oneself insensible to what the actor—given opportunity—can do. To make him part of a picture, however cunningly our attention is focused on that part, is to give him only the fraction of an opportunity. But what more in this kind can the movie do for him which will not be to the prejudice of the picture as a whole? And "registered" speech assimilated to the picture must be under like limitations. It comes to this, I think. Accomplishments of all sorts can be reproduced; but the human factor in the theater involves something more. The power of the actor over his audience rests for a very short while upon his looks, nor to a great extent upon how skilfully he does what he has to do; for longer, perhaps, on the magnetism of his speech. Ultimately it seems to rest upon something that he *is*. Other qualities may attract an audience, but it is by this that he will hold them. Can the movie find means—as it must—by which he can exercise this power to the full at second hand? That is the question. And this personal factor—to return, momentarily, to the educative aspect of the drama—dominates, of course, much more than the drama. It is, in fact, the key to the working of all human relations. Can the movie be imagined exemplifying it?

THE ACTOR'S STANDPOINT

Actors will inevitably be most concerned with the ephemeral aspect of the drama, since their own stake in it, however distinguished, must be (I have contended) of this particularly mortal kind. The drama, complete in its acting, has more of the attributes of life itself than has any other art; and, like life, it passes. But there is the other aspect, its credit built up over the years by the accumulation—and by time's selection—of a body of plays which have had in them an enduring worth and vitality. Except for these and the standard they set, the actor's art would still be abiding at about the level of the *commedia dell' arte*. It finds its higher ranges only in such plays as these. And—for a parallel—consider what the credit of a musician would be if he contented himself and thought to content his audience with nothing but the music that is written today to be forgotten tomorrow.

A theater—again, not a theater building, but an organization by which the art of the drama can be cultivated—should enshrine these two aspects of it, of the plays to be performed, of the art of their presentation; and its value will lie in the reconciling of the two. Material equipment must be adequate, if only for economy's sake; but primarily it will be an association of men and women cooperating in the practice of an art. Discipline will be needed. In no comparable activity is it needed more. And nowhere, one may add, is it more likely to be found—despite vulgar report to the contrary —than in a well-organized theater. But it must be self-discipline. For there is a danger in organizing any art, that of organizing the free spirit by which it lives—its peculiar virtue—out of existence altogether. One must beware of mere efficiency. The aim here would be to develop in the theater and its company that best sort of comradeship, which belongs to the good regiment, the good government, the good school or university, in which individual pride becomes pride in the whole, by which the value of the whole comes mysteriously to exceed that of the sum of the parts. And whenever this semi-miracle is achieved the effect will perhaps be more notable in a body of artists working happily together than in any other collection of fallible human beings.

THE DRAMA OF ENDURING WORTH

The main problem for such a theater as we are envisaging (but it is the problem of all institutions) would lie in the combining of stability and vitality. Its stability would let it be in some sort a guardian of that drama of enduring worth upon which, as we said, the prestige of the art of the theater ultimately rests. It could save plays of this quality from oblivion; its company would put their vitality to the proof. It could enlarge the scope of the drama's general appeal, triply limited as this now is, by the sort of play acted, in the way it commonly is acted, in the narrow section of the public appealed to. Doubtless our purveyors of theatrical fare are ever assiduously seeking the "new idea"—which need be neither so new nor very much of an idea—and variety at any cost. But when this is found it usually proves to be only superficial, shop-window, variety, behind which the old monotony persists. The actors are still called on to sound—to a slightly different tune perhaps—the same few, well-worn notes, out of the wide gamut of expression that they could command; the comic, which "gets a laugh," the erotic, the pathetic, which, dwelt on, earns an occasional sniff. But if these are all to which the ear and the taste of an audience are attuned the rest may as well be left dumb. Why should an actor—and how can he!—cultivate to the fullest an art that he is only called on to exercise so crudely and scrappily? Let him follow where popularity leads and learn only what applause can teach him. He will be "successful," no doubt, but with half his capacities coarsened by over-use, and the rest atrophied for lack of any.

THE THEATER'S THIRD FACTOR: THE AUDIENCE

As to the audience,

The drama's laws the drama's patrons give,
And we, who live to please, must please to live.

Lickspittle doctrine, and likely to encourage—Johnson might have stopped to consider—only such drama as he himself, from his seat in the pit, would have damned at sight. It is futile to appeal to public taste for a lead. That will lead nowhere, since the public *has* no taste—no more positive taste, let us say, than has been taught it by dramatists and actors and ratified by a critic or two; and even so it arrives at nothing more specific than a Yes or No. There are various sorts of audience, yet not very variously composed. Hamlet and his kin have a place in most, and could rewrite the play; and they know just how it should be acted. Polonius will certainly be there. He, if you remember, did enact Julius Caesar in the university once; now, by the time we meet him, "he is for a jig or a tale of bawdry, or he sleeps." But appeal will be mainly made to the presumed majority, who expect entertainment and as much excitement as will digest their latest meal. Though there is nothing wrong about that, there comes to be about nothing but that; moreover, if the entertainer makes such entertainment his sole and direct aim, he becomes, by confident repetition, likelier to miss than to hit it.

The pervading difficulty in the theater lies in the close interdependence—in no cooperative art is this closer—of its several factors. A play must have a fitting company of actors; together they must have a fitting audience too. And these three factors—this is the crux of the matter— must find themselves in simultaneous and all but unanimous accord. A play may appeal but to a minority of its potential public, its actors cannot to a minority of a particular audience; they might be left acting, before the play ended, to a minority of one—or less! To the enlarging of the scope of the drama, then, to an enhancing of its quality, all three factors must contribute, each as it can; and what one may try to do without the other two, or two without the third, will be largely wasted effort. The history of the theater, distant and recent, records a gallant and ever-hopeful succession of these transient and incomplete efforts, soon forgotten, except by the theatrical historian, who must collect such uncertain memories of them as he may. Only the dramatist can in the nature of things leave some preciser record of his work behind him, his share in the whole, from which the whole—the play in full being—can be brought to life again. We justly speak of "reviving" a play.

THE PAST WHICH IS NO PAST

During the four hundred years and more of the modern drama's existence many plays of many sorts have been written. Most of them, no doubt, were—as most plays are today—imitations of imitations of what was not worth imitating to begin with, never had much more life in them than was given them by their first actors, and certainly would not respond to any attempt to revive them. Then there are the plays, still full enough of vitality, but written to be of more or less topical interest. Are these worth reviving? Are they capable of real revival? Can we, with the best will in the world, come to appreciate the wit-combats of *Love's Labours Lost*? Luckily the speech about the King's Evil in *Macbeth* is easily omitted. Do we genuinely enjoy *Les Précieuses Ridicules*? How much do we not inevitably miss of the satire of *An Enemy of the People*?

But a very small change turns "topical" into "historical" interest, and that can be a positive addition to a play's value nowadays. Never, I suppose, has a sense of the past been more widely cultivated and under so many guises as in the last few decades. Various aspects of history, political, social, economic; biographies by the hundred; diaries; correspondence; facts fictionalized and frank fiction; centenaries celebrated weekly—have we ever shown such interest in our ancestors before? It is easily explicable. We stand at a fateful juncture in the world's history, and we are at this very moment pledging ourselves—we democratic nations in particular—to be more prudent shepherds of its future than we have proved in the past. No better reason is needed for our interest in that past, and in other than the doings of its kings and ministers; since it will not be in their hands only but as much and more in ours, strengthening them, that the fortunes of the future, we believe, will lie.

Its nature allowed for, there is no better witness to the

life and temper of the past than the drama of the time. It varies in kind. *Bartholomew Fair, Love, for Love, The Enemy of the People*, are pictures of such sections of life as the theater can easily accommodate. They are seen, of course, through the eyes and colored by the humors of Jonson and Congreve and Ibsen; but these were not unreliable interpreters, and contemporary audiences seem to have recognized a likeness to life. Shakespeare's Histories and Roman plays provide, naturally, no evidence of how the Wars of the Roses were actually fought or Antony betrayed and self-betrayed; and the theater could not in any case accommodate more than mere symbols of such events. But they tell us what Shakespeare, and the public he swayed, thought and felt about these things, about kingship and empire and the passions they nourish. And this is perhaps even more worth the knowing.

Students of history, no doubt, gain something indirectly by simply reading the plays. But unless they are students of drama, too, this will be of uncertain benefit; and even when they are, of no more—to use a worn comparison—than is a music-student's reading of a score, while he might be hearing it performed. Nor, in any case, is an art something to be cultivated for the sole benefit of its students. The language of music and drama, and of painting and sculpture, should be a part of the cultural currency of the educated world.

The drama's incomparable vividness—its pictures painted in the human medium of the actors—lends to the past the actuality of the present. Also it sets us asking:

when does the past begin? By the clock, it is beginning as I speak these words. But of what does the past consist? By less mechanical measurement, of the things we have done with. And what is still active for us and within us is therefore not to be reckoned in that sort of past at all. There is a famous line in Jonson's tribute to the dead Shakespeare—"He was not for an age but for all time"— which we commonly read as conventional hyperbole (to which, incidentally, Jonson was not very prone). But it can be given an exacter meaning; and, certainly, three centuries and a half of time by the clock have told little on his value to us.

THE EXEMPLARY CASE OF SHAKESPEARE

Shakespeare did not write such plays as *Bartholomew Fair*. He preferred to set his scene in times or places where his imagination could range more freely. Yet he would give its figures familiar traits so as to bring them home to us and thus create that combination of the actual and the highly imagined in which lay his unique strength. Hamlet's Elsinore is no far cry from the London of its staging. Bottom the Athenian weaver and Dogberry the constable of Messina might be met at the next street corner. Oswald, the sycophant upstart from about the court of King James is posted back intact into the England of King Lear; and Cleopatra wears a stomacher and plays billiards. These incongruities passed unremarked, since (apart from his audience's carelessness about such matters) the life of the characters lay, not in these circumstantial things but in the ideas and emotions informing them, which, whether or no they prove valid for "all time," are certainly so—and have already proved so—for more than one place and age. It is astonishing how little out of touch with Shakespeare and his age we are. Upon certain questions the Elizabethans felt as we no longer do, about kingship and its privileges, for instance; nor are we haunted, as they were, by the memory of a thirty-year civil war. If we are to appreciate the Histories we must take with us to the theater a little historical sense—but a very little will serve. We do not think about witches quite as Macbeth did, nor about ghosts as did Hamlet. But his feelings about his mother and uncle would be ours, and his spiritual doubts and misgivings make a pattern (as we said) for many a man's today. Nor does it take modern costume to make the politics of Coriolanus modern.

What are the qualities in Shakespeare's plays that do most to keep them alive today? He was no faultless artist nor great philosopher nor, by direct means, a moral teacher; and devout attempts to fasten these titles on him fail. But he was a most remarkable observer; his mind like a sensitive plate, faithfully registering every impression it received. And he was a poet—which meant among other things that his eyes saw what commoner eyes could not see, beauties they missed, and, beneath the surface, into men's secret thoughts and motives. He lived and wrote at a time, too, when there was unusually much of this sort to be divined. For it was one of England's most revolutionary and formative ages, when the full effect of the belated impact of the Renaissance was first felt there, and men, in a freshly kindled awareness, were trying to come to a freer understanding of the world and themselves. Since then we may seem to have changed in much. We have—in the clothes we wear and the way we live. The world has changed. Air travel and radio now have their part in its organizing. England is no longer a mere little island but the hub of a great commonwealth, and the vast *terra incognita* somewhere to the west of those "still vext Bermoothes" has become "these United States." We have changed in the things we *do*: but how little yet those things have changed us in what we *are*, in our ways of thinking, our moral standards, the religions we profess, our weekday creeds besides. And these are the things, with which—comically colored, tragically intensified—Shakespeare's genius dealt. And we are much the same men. Caius Marcius and Menenius and the Tribunes are in politics still; and Hotspur (if without his blank verse) and Fluellen and probably Pistol are to be found on every battlefield: Yet change may be upon us, more of a change than lies in dress and travel and talk. A clever invention or so will not effect it; but men's view of the world and of themselves does change. Medieval man—we may call him so; the man of the Crusades—gave way in time to Renaissance man, whose kingdom, to which we have belonged, may now in turn be giving way to another, built upon six or seven generations of an ever-encroaching industrial, mechanical, scientific civilization, culminating in two world wars. What the spiritual product of this will be—what type of man will emerge from its marvelous confusions—we do not yet know. Despite history's warnings he may be for utter revolution, and may put very much more than Shakespeare behind him and among those things of the past that he has definitely done with. And in times of catastrophe such changes come rapidly; so not a few of us now living may live to see such a change.

ENDURING ART

There are those of us, however, who cling to our heritage meanwhile, believing in the continuity of man's long progress—no matter the stumbling—up from the beast, in today's debt, therefore, to yesterday, and in the value to the present of that still living past, which is not past. Art of all sorts has a dominant share in keeping that past alive, in making it a part of the present. Think. A tune is played centuries ago, a sequence of notes breathed into the air, no more than that; or a poet writes a verse. Melody and verse are still alive today. Drama, as we said, is generously privileged in this. And if it can vivify the past—which is not past—for our present, it can equally preserve the present for the future. The good play of today will have its vital value for tomorrow also.

With this, then, we clinch the claims of a true theater to a worthy place in the world. It can, as no other art can, help to keep us vividly conscious of the continuity of our civilization. And without this continuity, without, what is more, the consciousness of it, is it too much to say that no civilization can survive? The theater also serves its purpose the better because all parties concerned must collaborate in the work. The dramatist does his share once and for all; today—or if done yesterday, that serves for today. The actor's contribution is continually renewable, and should, to his audience, seem ever to be freshly made. This presents him with a problem in the practice of his art that he shares, indeed, with every interpreter: how to combine mastery of his material with apparent spontaneity in the use of it. The problem may be insoluble in its entirety. It would occur in such a theater as we have been envisaging, for it belongs to the finer aspects of the art. I do not attempt to deal with it, and I have refrained from speaking, except incidentally, about the art of acting at all. Frankly, the subject is too exasperating. Historical events have assembled here, and you are assimilating, the finest material for the making of actors, in variety of race and temperament at least, that can ever have been seen. And what is the opportunity offered the would-be actor for his art's development? The nightly repeating, if he is lucky, of a few effective tricks of self-display, which he will attach to one character after another; and the fewer the characters he is called on to interpret the luckier a career his will be. If that sounds too sweeping a condemnation, allow me a last comparison with the musician and his music. An actress will cheerfully walk on the stage to play Rosalind or Cleopatra with not one-tenth of the equipment in mere skill that a pianist must acquire before venturing in public upon the simplest sonata or concerto. Again: keep a master of the violin playing only puerile stuff year after year, and how long will his mastery endure? Yet again: Tchaikovsky is a most attractive composer in his way, so are Offenbach and Sullivan in theirs. But perform at concert after concert nothing except their work—or, worse, imitations of it—and where, very soon, will your musical public be? Where, moreover, would musical criticism be, and, after a while, where the musicians themselves? Doubtless the century-old round of "classic" plays and parts, in which every aspiring actor once had to prove his quality, came to be wearisome, to audience and critics and even to the actors themselves. But in the acting of Hamlet or Benedick there was a standard of ability to be reached or surpassed, even as there is now for the playing of the Emperor concerto. Within that accustomed round the audience became qualified as critics, and the actor's art as a thing in itself had some meaning for them. For acting is not to be judged merely by the emotional effect it may happen to make upon the less sophisticated among us; and critical enjoyment of it is of the keener kind by far.

The part to be played by a critical audience is a passive but important one. Its obligations are simple: to go to the theater, now and then, otherwise disposed than for mere digestive entertainment and no more; to learn to like things which are good of their sort, whatever the sort, and to submit to no others. Some small amount of learning is involved; but the essentials of it can be slipped almost unnoticed into the regular course of our education, with appreciation of the arts in general admitted once more, as it is, to be a part of this. From which standpoint it is that I have been trying to discuss the use of the drama, a use depending from first to last upon our treatment of it as a normal, sane and ordinary activity, into which may sometimes be breathed extraordinary life and beauty and spiritual power.

Postscript

I HAVE DONE. You may, it occurs to me, find something incongruous in a discussion of art at a time when this most destructive of wars is still raging. You cannot, believe me, find it more incongruous than I do. But artists and men of letters must resign themselves under such conditions either to going ahead with their own work and admitting its momentary uselessness or to finding other sorts of work altogether—which they will probably do worse than the next man. The personal aspect of the matter is, of course, not important, except to the one person. But to be of no present use and to have to remember that the past is of no real interest—for all their polite protests—to younger people who have never known it is to find oneself driven forward upon the future; even though one's juniors may then reasonably retort, "As you will never know that, what concern is it of yours?" I pray their forbearance. These speculations are all they leave us to play with. It is possible, too, that our experience—which is the name we give to the record of our mistakes—may be of some indirect use to them, as a shadowy bridge between past and future. We elders look, according to our natures and moods, sometimes a little wistfully, sometimes, for their sakes, a little ruefully toward that future.

THE COMING PEACE

I have never doubted that we should win this war, though God knows I had no right to take for granted the devotion of the fighting men who are winning it. Even had we British been left to fight it out alone I should still have foreseen, at the worst in some far future, on some remote mountain, another Cave of Covadonga, in which a band of Christian knights would gather for such another eight hundred years' struggle as expelled the Moslem from Spain. The world does not go backwards in its tracks. Our fight has been a fight for the future of Christian civilization, and it was bound to be won. Which of us could dare doubt that? But what of the peace? We are devising, to enable us to keep it, better machinery than ever before. That is needed, no doubt; but of itself it will effect nothing. Its utility depends on the worth of the men who are to work it, upon our worth, and, if we mean to continue in our democratic way of life, upon the worth and wisdom of every single one of us; for that is democracy's ultimate implication. Well, not only apparently do we mean to, but we mean to shepherd other nations also into this way of life, or help restore them to it when they have lapsed from grace. We speak sometimes of "re-educating" them. There is a certain complacency in the notion which should prompt us to a little self-questioning. Is our own education so sound, our civilization so complete that we can be content to impose them, as they are, upon other peoples? Certainly we have high ideals, and, in providing for the world's peace, the very best intentions—but these can make hell's pavement, as we know. On the other hand, it is idle for the sceptical critic to recommend us to perfect our own ways before we set about correcting other people's. The world will not stand still for that. But we can give more urgent thought than we have ever given yet to our shortcomings in this kind; and perhaps, with this crucial task ahead of us, we had better do so—while there is still time. The victors in a war are not as a rule very apt at self-examination. For ten years after the last war I lived in France, a country I love much. The French custom was to speak of November 11, not as Armistice day, the day, as we then thought it was, of deliverance, but as *le Jour de la Victoire*. There was nemesis in the very words. Victory this time is to lay on us an even greater responsibility than that we shouldered, and let slip twenty-five years ago. Shall we be equal to it? That is a grim question.

DEMOCRACY IN THE MAKING

If we cannot make something finer of our democratic society than we have already made of it the answer may be bluntly: No. Democracy, as it is today, can hardly be called the last word in civilization. We shall be wiser to think of ours as a democracy still in the making. It has given us the forms of freedom, but these do not of themselves make us free. We are at present meshed in the machinery of many marvelous inventions; but these, we see only too clearly, cannot of themselves civilize us, and they may but empower us to be the greater brutes. The use of freedom must be learnt, and civilization is nowhere if not within us. It is all a question of learning how to live, of education. Wherever we turn for a solution of our problems, political, industrial, or social, we find ourselves—do we not?—returning to this question

[89]

of education. The importance of it was soon seen, and the dangers that lay in an uneducated democracy. During the past century or so we have done something to modify them; but the dangers that lie in a half-educated democracy, which may think itself educated, are perhaps greater still. And the problems of the world's immediate future center here; since, if force is not to control it intellect must, intellect and that less definable thing which we call "character." Unanimously we now demand education. We are less agreed upon an answer to the question: what education *is*. A snowball of a notion has been set rolling—has rolled up already to a monstrous size and is hard to stop—that it consists in the accumulating of information about a lot of things we do not understand. Have we to learn over again what education *is* by dint of learning what it is *not*? As to the cultivating of character, that, of course, takes generations, the individual, meanwhile, acquiring a little humility, and some respect for the past.

My business with you—and thank you for your patience —has been to discuss the use of the arts in education, and of one in particular, the art of the drama. You will have gathered, I hope, that I do not see much use in encouraging the average adolescent student of the humanities to give time and energy to the actual practice of the arts, painting, sculpture, music or the drama. No harm need result, some good may; but any genuine vocation will almost certainly have made itself heard before this, and will not need encouragement. And when we consider what sort of man or woman we want our education to produce—for all lies there—it will quite certainly not be the disappointed aesthete. We want, I suppose, in the citizens of our new world natures cultivated to be suitably articulate, keenly critical, fully appreciative. If we are to remain, in any true sense, individualists and democrats, it is the quality of the individual that matters most to us. And if democracies are to guide the world, they must be represented, not so much by the "common man," as by uncommon men; the common man made uncommon. Keep the standard high, and there will never be too many. The arts help us here; and our question has been: how best to bring the influence of one among them to bear upon education, with due regard to its own lively dignity, and without prejudice to what it can come to mean to a man for the rest of his life. That is the problem. Art is not mere entertainment, although it can be most entertaining. It is a moral exercise, although it need never be depressingly solemn. It should leaven the daily life of a community. It frees men's imagination, and controls it. If it is of good quality itself it sets a standard of quality, even in the simplest things. Quality is its watchword. There will be the difference between a nature it influences and one to which it means nothing that is the difference between crude iron and tempered steel.